How To Do Things You Hate:

Self-Discipline to Suffer Less, Embrace the Suck, and Achieve Anything

By Peter Hollins,

Author and Researcher at peterhollins.com

Table of Contents

Chapter One: "What's Wrong with Me?!"

You wake up a little late one morning, and you're completely exhausted. You have a scary-looking to-do list, and you're exhausted just looking at it. Eventually you pull yourself out of bed, force yourself to get ready for the day, and cajole yourself into doing the day's tasks much the same way an armed prison warden watches over a chain gang to make sure that nobody is slacking off.

But you still manage to slack off anyway, and after barely five minutes on a task, you already notice your mind popping up and asking you if it's time for a break. Then a whole slew of well-worn excuses come out of the woodwork: It's too late to get started now anyway, you're tired (actually, come to think of it, do you feel a little cold coming on . . .?), and truthfully you don't really even know what you're doing. You can do this later, or maybe you don't have to do it at all.

Fast forward a few minutes and you're scrolling mindlessly online or doing some other nonessential task ("the spice rack *urgently* needed to be alphabetized; what else was I going to do?"). Even worse, maybe you're doing that special kind of "relaxing" that doesn't actually feel relaxing at all—i.e., you're avoiding the work you said you'd do but getting very little joy from it, because you now feel guilty, anxious, and resentful about the whole thing. Not much of a break when you know that the dreaded task is still waiting there for you in the wings, right?

Through a massive exertion of willpower, you manage to turn away from whatever screen is distracting you and push yourself to focus on the task again. It feels boring, pointless, too hard. You grind through, putting every last bit of effort into it . . . and five minutes later you stop again. By the end of the day, you've done very little but somehow feel absolutely spent. The next morning, your to-do list is a little longer and a little scarier . . .

If this problem sounds at all familiar, then you've probably asked yourself this question: What on earth is wrong with me?!

One possible answer is: **you're lazy.**

The thing about diagnosing this complex string of behaviors as laziness is that it's, well . . . lazy. Whether you call it procrastination, fear of failure, laziness, or fatigue, something is holding you back and preventing you from achieving the goal you have already identified for yourself as valuable. The instinct may be to run from the problem, but in doing so, you never get to understand why you behave this way in the first place. In fact, as you read on, you may come to see that this overly simplistic and knee-jerk labeling of behavior as "lazy" is part of precisely the same set of beliefs and habits that keeps you behaving this way!

So we will begin our book not with, say, ten easy productivity hacks for getting over your laziness, but rather a closer look at what laziness actually *is*. **You procrastinate for a reason. Understand that reason and you give yourself a real chance to do something different.** On the other hand, if you are uninterested in *why* you behave as you do right now, you may very well stay trapped there, constantly trying to solve a problem using the very same mindset that created the problem in the first place.

The Different Types of Laziness

So let's take a curious, neutral, almost scientific attitude to the problem. First, what is laziness?

Laziness can be defined as the conscious unwillingness to put in the necessary effort required for a task, encompassing both mental and physical exertion. People are often lazy even though they know that being so will create problems for them, whether that's more work to do later, missed opportunities, or negative feelings.

There is no fixed psychological definition of laziness (although it has been associated with lower measures on one of the "Big Five" personality traits: conscientiousness). Perhaps that's because **what we call laziness is actually a cluster of behaviors, beliefs, attitudes, habits, and emotions**. Laziness often overlaps with but is distinct from:

- Procrastination
- Lack of motivation
- Depression
- Lack of self-control
- Inability to resist distractions

- Certain attitudes to both the goal and the effort required
- Faulty self-concept

Furthermore, laziness is not just a result of these many complicated variables, it also acts as a trigger for secondary behaviors, thoughts, and feelings. We might feel shame or criticize ourselves or take our behavior as confirming evidence that we are a hopeless case because there is something intrinsic in our nature that makes us lazy.

If you've been battling laziness for a long time, it can feel counterintuitive to face these feelings and examine them more closely, but doing so is the only way to really understand what is happening. Avoiding these uncomfortable truths about the way we think and feel currently tends to block us from deeper insight into the problem ... and finding a way to transform ourselves once and for all.

Your laziness (for lack of a better word) is unique to you, and that means that the way you get better will also be unique to you. Luckily, all you need to find this unique solution is an open mind, a little curiosity, and the willingness to have some self-compassion. Later in the book we will absolutely explore different methods for cultivating good habits, discipline, and mental fortitude. But the first step to doing all that is to be okay with who and where we are right now, without shame and avoidance.

As you read through the following "types" of laziness (they are more like underlying *causes* of laziness), see if you can recognize yourself in any of them. You may relate to more than one.

Confusion
"I don't know what to do."

You know *that* you should do something, but you don't know *what* that should be. Let's say you're in the process of building a new business, but you've never done it before. You have some unclear ideas about building a website, so you put some vague item on your to-do list called "website," but what does that even mean? You sit down to work, but you're aimless and unsure. You end up feeling more and more anxious (perhaps even feeling stupid or incompetent), and you just end up avoiding the task or giving up.

You're not lazy—you're confused! You don't know what is expected of you or what the next step is. This may overlap with a question of poor planning and organization, as well as a lack of clarity about your specific role.

Quick solution: Take a step back and acknowledge the lack of clarity. Take time to reflect and gather the necessary information. Get comfortable with the fact that you will first need to ask questions to dispel the confusion—only then can you start acting. In this example, you could arrange a meeting with a business coach to help you clarify your goals and overall strategy. Then you get to work outlining a plan of action so you're not as bewildered anymore.

Fear
"I can't do it."

Fear can paralyze you. Fear in this context is a reaction to what we *expect* to happen once we take action. We avoid setting up our website, for example, because we're afraid that it will look awful, that people won't visit it, that we'll do it wrong, that we or others will discover that we are actually big ol' frauds.

The thing about this kind of fear is that it is not based in reality (i.e., in the here and now) but in fantasy (i.e., the future, or at least what we are imagining the future to be). In its own strange way, neurotic fear is trying to protect you from an outcome that you have decided is undesirable. Many people can't act because they're trying to avoid a perceived negative outcome, but occasionally you may be trying to avoid a perceived positive outcome. Maybe achieving your goal would force you to reconsider your self-concept as a person who is always a failure. Success can be scary! Allowing procrastination to keep us stunted may not feel great, but it does have a certain comfortable predictability about it.

Quick solution: Don't avoid the fear; embrace it. Look at it square on and decide that it can be whatever it wants to be—but that it will never be a reason to not act. In other words, separate action from how you feel—you can always act, regardless of how you feel. Being scared is not dangerous, and there is no need for it to stop you from doing anything.

We'll look at this in much more depth later, but for now, a great way to reduce the power you give to fear is to take actions, but keep them small. Take a baby step. Then when you're done, take another. But only focus on the baby step just in front of you, nothing else. Prove to yourself that you can be scared and act anyway. This builds confidence (and usually shows you just how unfounded the fears actually were).

Fixed Mindset
"I can't fail."

Closely related to the fear of failure is the fear of making mistakes or looking stupid to others. You might unconsciously feel like you can't act because you will look a bit stupid at first, and being "lazy" spares you the embarrassment. For example, someone might have a dream to write a novel, and believe they have the talent and intelligence to do so. But when they produce a few chapters, they realize that they are very much an awkward beginner and not already a fully-fledged author after their first attempt.

Their next step might be to share their first draft and ask for feedback, but this is embarrassing. Instead, they give up on the idea completely. For the rest of their lives, they may say, "I have a novel in me. One day I'll write it, when I have the time." But the limiting factor is not time—that's an excuse. The real problem is they are unwilling to endure the *learning process* that becoming a good writer entails.

This is called a fixed mindset—the belief that talent and intelligence are inborn and unchanging. In other words, you're either a good writer or you're not. The consequence of this mindset is that when you encounter any evidence that you're not a good writer, you give up. You have disregarded the possibility of learning. A growth mindset, on the other hand, sees talents and skills as things you develop. Being a beginner who makes mistakes, then, is not an impediment to achievement but the actual path you take to achievement.

Quick solution: Stop telling yourself that you can't fail, or refuse to fail. Stop telling yourself that you're brilliant and smart. This is not motivational—it's fragile thinking. Rather, tell yourself that "failure" is just a necessary part of becoming better. In fact, reframe failure as learning, and challenge as opportunity. *Expect* to not know how to do things. Detach your ego from the process. In our example, if you notice your first chapter sucks, get professional feedback and take it without thinking that it means anything about your worth as a person.

Fatigue
"I'm too exhausted. I don't have the energy to do it."

Let's first just say that of course it's possible to be too tired to act. We are human beings with human limits on our energetic resources. Rest is necessary. That said, a big portion of our *perception* of lethargy is purely psychological. We all have different ways of noticing and interpreting neutral signals of mental or physical tiredness. We cannot change hard physiological limits, but we can change the meanings we ascribe to our changing energy levels.

Let's say you have to read and summarize a chapter of a textbook one morning. But you're tired. You tell yourself, "I'm so sleepy. I can't do it," and so you don't. But this is a disempowering and passive way of looking at things. A more proactive and empowered approach would be to accept that you will occasionally feel tired, to embrace it, and to work with it. Doing so allows you to acknowledge the fact that you're not tired for some random, mysterious reason . . . you've been going to bed past midnight for a week.

Quick solution: What is your fatigue telling you? Allow that to guide conscious action. If your lifestyle needs tightening up, then do that. Eat better, sleep, take more breaks. Take a moment to reappraise any expectations of yourself—are they realistic? Finally, you might actually not be tired at all, but rather avoidant, fearful, etc. Take a look at this feeling of fatigue and get curious about what it is telling you. If you're genuinely shattered and can't manage a full chapter, that's fine. Accept that you're tired. Do half a chapter. Try again tomorrow.

Apathy
"I couldn't care less."

"It doesn't even matter."

Apathy is actually a mask—underneath that mask of passivity is aggression, anger, hostility, defiance, and resentment. Do not ignore this feeling, since it can point to a real lack of alignment with your goals, or even to the fact that your goals are not the right ones for you. The defiance hidden in apathy is often nothing more than old warnings that have gone unheeded, and boundaries that have been repeatedly violated—by yourself or others.

Apathy *can* be a sign of depression, but in this context it's better understood as one of its causes. Imagine the example of someone who has been encouraged to pursue an elite athletic career from childhood. They eventually may start hating the sport not because they're not good at it or can't do it, but because it's not truly their motivation to do it—it's a motivation that belongs to other people.

Quick(-ish) solution: Re-evaluate your principles and values. Go back to the drawing board to check that this current goal is in alignment with those. You may have lost excitement for the goal just because you've lost touch with the vision and purpose that inspired it in the first place. But it also may be that you are angry because you don't actually want the goal—and when you say "I don't care," it's because, well, you don't. What do you care about? Get curious about *that* goal.

Self-Belief

"I'm just a lazy person. I've always been like that."

Are you constantly telling yourself and others that you lack patience, discipline or motivation? When a fixed mindset really beds in, it becomes a permanent part of your identity. To say that underachieving is *who you are* is just about the most self-limiting thing you can do! This is because you have then defined any action, growth, or improvement as an existential threat—as literally something that will change who you are.

Quick solution: Don't overly identify with fleeting thoughts or emotions. Mindfulness meditation can help here. If you feel lazy one day, that doesn't mean you are a lazy person and that this one day defines you as a human being. Accept that you can be many different ways, but that this doesn't necessarily say anything about you, and it especially doesn't control what action you can take. That means that just because you've had a few lazy days, it doesn't mean that you are doomed by fate to wake up today and be lazy again. You can always choose. You never need to create a character for yourself and limit yourself to only behaving as you think that character should behave.

Loss of Heart

"Everything's such a mess right now, it doesn't matter if I do it or not."

This kind of laziness is less about fixed mindset and lack of self-belief, and more about discouragement and loss of hope. Feeling like a bit of a victim can seriously undermine your motivation to act. You have lost belief that your actions can have a reasonable effect on the world, so why bother?

Quick solution: For this one, there is no quick solution, but it will help to forcefully drop the "poor me" attitude. Make the Serenity Prayer your new mantra (actually, just tattoo it on your chest so you never, ever forget it!): "Grant me the serenity to accept the things I cannot change, the courage to change the things I can, and the wisdom to know the difference." Loss of heart can arise when we have allowed our attention to remain too long on the things we actually cannot control. The way out is to teach yourself to focus on what can be fixed, and to gracefully accept what was never in your zone of control in the first place.

Comfort Orientation
"I'll do it . . . after I do this other fun thing."

The previous seven types of laziness are, in fact, not laziness at all. But this final one is: It is simply the tendency to prefer comfort and convenience over exertion and effort. That's it. "Pure" laziness—and we're all capable of it.

It's not a serious mental health diagnosis or a major existential problem to solve. This is the kind of laziness that arises because on some level you have decided that watching entertaining videos on YouTube is more fun than making the week's budget, so that's what you'll do. It's the valuing of comfort and ease over even the smallest exertion or inconvenience.

Quick solution: Stop doing that! There's no big psychoanalytic theory you need to understand about human nature; there's no major trauma in your childhood to unpack. This form of laziness is just laziness, and the only solution is necessarily one that will be a bit inconvenient and uncomfortable. If you are lucky, this will be the only form of laziness you have to face in your life. It's lucky because the solution is really simple: Activate your willpower, take action, and be disciplined. Not *easy*, no, but simple!

Before we move on, pause for a moment and see if you can identify which forms of laziness are most evident in your own life—it's likely to be a mix. It's also important to separate out the underlying psychological causes for your behavior, from simple comfort orientation (i.e., really just being lazy). This is because the approaches for each are different and mutually exclusive. If you're not sure, tune into your own radio station for a few days (i.e., listening to your self-talk) and notice what reasons/excuses you give for not acting. Also notice the primary emotions you feel, as these can hint at the type of laziness you're experiencing.

The Five Hindrances to Self-Mastery

So, to conclude, the answer to the question "What's wrong with me?" is: "Probably lots of different things"!

You might be failing to act because of apathy, fear, genuine exhaustion, poor lifestyle choices, bad planning and organization, anger and resentment, not being aligned with your goals, feeling hopeless or powerless, lacking self-belief, or simply not believing that acting is within your identity. Or it could be because you're lazy, in the most ordinary sense of the word.

We've considered a few "quick solutions," but really, **there is only one overarching solution for most laziness problems, and it's not discipline, but self-mastery.**

The concept of self-discipline is intricately related to the journey of understanding our purpose and achieving self-mastery. It involves making a commitment to building patience, discipline, and self-awareness. This commitment is essential in various areas of life, including the pursuit of goals, personal development, and even in the practice of disciplines like martial arts. It applies to you whether your issues come from long-standing psychological roadblocks, from plain old comfort orientation, or from a mix of both.

Shaolin monks know a thing or two about self-mastery. In the context of becoming a Shaolin master, the individual in question dedicates around thirty years to studying and practicing the interaction between mind and body. This pursuit aligns with the principles of Shaolin martial arts culture and philosophy, which have been established for over 1,500 years.

Within this philosophy, an important teaching is the "five hindrances of self-mastery." These hindrances represent core mental states that hinder clear perception, wise decision-making, goal achievement, and a harmonious life. By recognizing and overcoming these hindrances, individuals can cultivate self-discipline and embark on the path of self-mastery.

In the West we tend to have a rather shallow conception of discipline, likening it to a fairly basic application of the will, or simply being strong enough to push against oneself. The practice of martial arts, such as Shaolin, requires discipline on multiple levels—and the wisdom to understand these levels in a more sophisticated way.

It's a life path that demands physical training to develop strength, agility, and technique, as well as mental training to enhance focus, concentration, and emotional control. Most likely, you're not a Shaolin monk, nor do you want to be one, but your life can be improved by adopting the same strategy.

Let's further increase our "laziness literacy" by understanding things from the Shaolin monk perspective. The Eastern perspective is less psychological and more about the philosophical, moral, and intellectual efforts required to live a wise, virtuous, and healthy life. The Shaolin monk, then, would say that **even though you may not be to blame for your current predicament, it is nevertheless your responsibility to find your way out of it**. Let's take a closer look.

Sensual Desire

Imagine you have been working diligently on a project with a tight deadline. However, you find yourself constantly distracted by the urge to snack on some chips you know are in the kitchen. Despite your initial intention to focus, the desire for sensory stimulation promised by those cheesy, crunchy chips pulls you away from your work.

Sensual desire is simply distraction via the channel of the senses—be it sights, sounds, touch, taste, or even smells. It can be the pleasure of sleep or rest, or preferring to be slouching, cozy, and warm at your desk rather than slightly cold and sitting upright.

To overcome sensual desire, one must counter the focus on the present moment and instead consider the long-term consequences of succumbing to sensual desires.

Your senses live in the present, and if you are continually focused on giving them what they want, you lose sight of the future and the *consequences* of indulging certain sensual distractions. Loosen the spell of the senses by fast forwarding your life and seeing what the outcome will be for each choice you make. If you get up three times from your work to munch on chips, the consequences are clear: You won't get your work done, you'll eat a snack that doesn't do anything for you nutritionally, and you'll probably feel bad about yourself afterward.

Now, compare *that* outcome with the bliss of eating those cheesy chips. Of course, there are advantages to living according to your senses. The question you have to learn to ask is whether those advantages outweigh not indulging. So you compare these two things:

1. The pain of letting yourself down, not doing your work, feeling guilty about it, losing time, and eating a calorific snack that's not really good for you.
2. The pain of knowing there are cheesy chips in the kitchen, and just . . . not eating them.

This is very different from comparing these two things:

1. The boredom of doing your work.
2. The deliciousness of the cheesy chips.

Note, however, this doesn't make the right choice easy. But it does show up the wrong choice for what it is, and hopefully make it less attractive.

Ill Will

Ill will is a mental state driven by strong dislike or rejection. It's the opposite of sensual desire because it's all about what you don't want. Ill will is the essence of resistance. We will look at how to better tolerate uncertainty and discomfort in a later chapter, but for now we'll just say that a big hindrance to self-mastery is the way we tend to avoid, reject, or judge certain things in life just because they are difficult.

This is a subtle point: Many of us have been taught that self-improvement is something that automatically has to feel good. We start to believe that if we are uncomfortable, bored, scared, or uncertain, that something is wrong and that we need to do whatever it takes to avoid those "negative feelings."

But really, negative feelings are just a part of life. Some things are hard to do. Struggling with them isn't a problem; it's just what it feels like to do that thing. Sometimes the real obstacle is just our own bad attitude! That means that:

The problem is not the person you're having an argument with, but your ill will—the avoidance of confronting them or setting boundaries.

The problem is not that your job is complicated and stressful, but your ill will— your unwillingness to endure that difficulty and work with it.

The problem is not that life is boring and your chores for the day are horrible, but your ill will—your belief that life ought to entertain you and that you are entitled always to pleasure and ease and nothing else.

To overcome ill will, explore new ways of approaching situations.

This may be as simple as reframing the way you interpret your experiences. For example, a young trainee will get walloped on the side of the head by his master during a combat exercise, and immediately think, "Ouch! What did I deserve that for? Stupid old man, that's not fair. He should go easier on me. I shouldn't get hurt in that way. Is this really what training is? Getting hit over and over again by someone who is better than me? I hate this; it's dumb."

Another trainee, however, might get walloped on the head and think, "Ouch, that really hurts. I am not going to let him have the chance to do *that* again."

For the first trainee, pain equals injustice, unfairness, and an unacceptable hardship, whereas for the second trainee, pain equals a valued teacher whose lesson can be heeded. Importantly, the pain is the same in both cases!

Sloth and Torpor

It may seem strange to Western ears to think of depression, hopelessness, and inertia in moralistic terms. But for the Shaolin monks, maintaining enthusiasm has a certain ethical dimension. It can even be seen as a duty or obligation—something that one learns to cultivate in precisely the same way one cultivates discipline or compassion. **In other words, remaining enthusiastic and motivated is not a state of mind that comes "for free," but something you have to actively and consciously develop.**

This is counter to what a lot of us secretly think. We may believe that if we're following our life purpose and doing what we genuinely want to do, that motivation will naturally result and we will be inspired to act. Actually, it's the other way around. We must first consciously choose to act toward our goals, and that will create and then sustain a feeling of motivation. When we act toward our goals, we create mini experiences that confirm our own agency, that strengthen our confidence, and that slowly add to our growing self-concept as a person who does those things. In this we find our motivation, and we can continue to act—a "virtuous cycle."

If you find you are slothful and unmotivated, try to think of it as a simple problem of lost momentum. The worst thing you can do is assume that your goal is somehow a bad fit for you or something that you don't truly want after all. It's more likely that you've simply allowed your motivational fire to burn too low—have you been dedicated to feeding it?

The solution for sloth and torpor is not to go out and find something flashy to help you rev your engines again—at best this can only be a short-term solution. Eventually that, too, will burn out, and you'll be back at square one again. Instead, the way out is simple: ACTION. If you are in a stagnant state, everything in you will push against this idea, but that's okay—you don't have to take quantum leaps. Commit only to a small action. Achieve it and notice how you have moved a little. Keep that momentum by taking the next small step. In this way, you gather speed and confidence.

Restlessness

The modern conception of this is the idea of "distraction" or a wandering mind. Mental restlessness means you fritter away energy on ruminations over things in the past or the future—and that means you have less available for real work right here in the present. Restlessness is the old problem of lack of focus—you become the diffused and weak beam of light rather than the laser-like beam that can cut through steel.

If anxiety, self-doubt, fear, and judgment take you out of the moment, the end result is indeed a kind of laziness. You set up a bad feedback loop: Because you are not in the present, you may make impulse decisions, miss important information, or fail to do your best. That creates more things to worry about or regret later on. It's a kind of self-fulfilling prophesy, with your mind constantly on the back foot, reacting to your life rather than acting from a position of agency and self-control.

Mindfulness meditation is not appropriate for every situation, but it is for this one. This will teach you to notice incoming stimuli and create enough psychological distance so that you can *choose* whether you want to engage with the thought or not.

Doubt and Skepticism

In more modern terms, lack of self-esteem or confidence, i.e., doubt in your abilities. This creates an anxious hesitation and self-negation that starts to undermine everything you do. You may be completely indecisive and miss out on opportunities, or spend so long in "analysis paralysis" that you're not even sure what you want anymore.

What's missing here is not discipline per se, but rather a sense of mental sturdiness: Self-doubt is the inability to trust yourself and the world at large, to take the leap of faith required to have strong convictions and follow them, and to truly commit to a path once you've chosen it.

Removing the Obstacles

As you can see, there are many different ways to conceptualize laziness, procrastination, and a lack of productivity. The "right" way is the way that helps you better understand your unique situation. However, we're exploring these various models not just because they're interesting on an abstract level, but because they help us decide what to do to solve the problem.

For the Shaolin monks, a four-step method was devised to remove the five obstacles they identified. You can use a version of this, called the RAIN method:

It stands for recognize, accept, investigate, and non-identification.

Recognize means to become aware of the state of mind you are currently in.

Accept means to acknowledge that this is in fact the case for you, and allow it to be the case without resistance, avoidance, judgment, or evaluation.

Investigate means to query this state of mind and understand it better. What caused it? What are the consequences of following through with it? Is it in alignment with your goals or values?

Non-identification means to recognize that the thoughts and feelings associated with this state of mind are something you are currently doing, but they are not who you *are*. "I am not my body. I am not my mind. I am not my thought. I am not my emotion." This creates some psychological distance, which then grants you a special power: the ability to consciously *choose* what you do next.

For example, you recognize that you are hankering after junk food. You accept and acknowledge this without getting distracted by blame or shame, or running away from the feeling. Instead you ask questions. "What's going on for me right now? Is this one of the five hindrances? What happens if I go down that path?" After a few moments' thought, you decide that, as tempting as it is, this thought is not something you want to engage with. It's no big deal. You're craving junk food, but cravings pass. You notice a brief spike of pretty intense desire and then a flash of anger at not fulfilling that desire . . . and then you notice it pass. You see that there is something beyond these fleeting experiences. You notice that you don't have to believe everything you say to yourself, and you don't have to blindly follow every impulse you have.

But here, a note on examples. The above is just a story, just a metaphor. Real life, as you're probably aware, is a lot more complicated. This is why reading about the techniques in this book will only get you so far—the magic happens you actively apply them to your own life. Then they will become three dimensional and far more real.

Master Shi Heng Yi told the following story in a TED talk:

> "A man was living close to a mountain and everyday he was thinking, how would it be to climb that mountain and what would I see on the peak?

> So finally the day came, and the man went on the journey.

> Arriving at the foot of the mountain, he met the first traveler. So he asked, 'How did you get up the mountain and what did you see at the top?'

> So the traveler shared his path and also the view that he had. But then the man was thinking, *The way that this traveler described to me sounds very exhausting. I need to find another way to climb.*

> So he continued to walk on the foot of the mountain until he met the next traveler. So once again he asked, 'How did you climb up that mountain and what did you see from the top?' And so again the traveler shared a story.

Still not being determined on which direction and which way to go, the man asked thirty more people, thirty more travelers. When he finished talking to all of them, he finally made up his mind.

'Now that so many people already shared with me their pasts and especially what they all saw from the top, I don't need to climb there anymore.' It is very unfortunate this man never went on the journey."

What this story tells us is that each of our journeys in life will be different. We are each too unique to learn about ourselves merely by copying others and the things they have learned. We need to actually go on the journey ourselves. Nobody can tell us what we will encounter on our journey, or how we can manage the challenges we'll find there. But people have been able to notice patterns in the kinds of things that tend to get in the way of every traveler—the five hindrances. **These hindrances are not events but states of mind or attitudes.** We each experience them in our lives, but the way we experience them will be unique to us. Self-mastery, then, is not a particular kind of life or a set of actions. It's an attitude and a *way* of living.

As you read through the rest of this book, bear in mind that some of the advice won't seem like it fits you or applies to your life. Try to remember that all the guidance offered here is like a series of road signs on the side of a mountain—they can point out various paths, obstacles, and hazards, but it's always YOU who has to navigate a unique path across that mountain. That happens beyond the pages of this book!

Understanding Experiential Avoidance

Welcome to the Roundabout

Take a look at the following scenarios and see if you can identify the common theme uniting them:

- You get an email from a colleague who makes a certain demand of you. Doing as they request is awkward and not something you really want to do, so you avoid responding for a few hours. Then there's an agitated follow-up email, and the awkwardness ramps up. But now you really don't want to get involved, so you reply but avoid properly answering any questions or actually doing what was asked. So you've avoided the first awkward but small task . . . and replaced it with a far bigger, more awkward task!

- You've been meaning to sign up for an important career development course. Because it's so important, you're intimidated. You put off signing up, then miss the first start date. A few months later you miss the second one, too. By the time the third course is starting up, you've worked yourself into a froth. Somehow, by trying to avoid committing yourself, you've become chained to this course that has hung over your head for almost a year.

- You have a project to submit, but you're afraid of failing and looking like an idiot. You procrastinate, then rush to finish the project at the last minute. You fail. Your supervisor tells you, "I don't understand. I know you know how to do this!"

There is one underlying mechanism in all these examples: **experiential avoidance** (EA). This is basically the world's worst coping mechanism. EA feels like a solution in the short term because it helps you avoid something unpleasant. But in doing so, you actually end up creating more of the feeling, because the problem tends to be deferred and made worse. This is why some psychologists term it a "roundabout"—you end up getting trapped, going around and around the same circle and never quite escaping it.

Here are two basic "rules" of life:

1. If you are alive, you will at some point encounter discomfort (in fact, you'll encounter it more if you're trying to grow and change).
2. People naturally want to avoid discomfort.

Herein lies a tension. You *want to* evolve and improve, but doing so requires you to do something you *don't want to do*: experience discomfort. One way to respond to this little snag is to tell yourself you want to achieve a goal, and then back away from it when it becomes uncomfortable. Then, in trying to control or avoid those difficult feelings, you find yourself suffering more. Round and round you go.

Avoidance comes in many shapes and sizes . . . and procrastination is just one of them.

Striving—being too busy, or an overachiever or a perfectionist

Numbing yourself—dulling negative feelings through substances and addictions

Tension—mentally and physically bracing yourself

Distraction—escaping into fantasy, denial, "multitasking"

Giving up—dropping out, isolating yourself, retreating, oversleeping

Rushing—blasting through things quickly as a way to avoid them

Intellectualizing—overthinking, analyzing

Procrastinating—putting things off, deferring, and dreading

This book is primarily about developing more discipline and self-mastery, but the effects of experiential avoidance go much further than productivity at work or setting goals for yourself. If you avoid the discomfort of emotionally heavy conversations, you lose the chance for more intimacy in your relationships. If you avoid the discomfort of critical feedback, you lose the chance to improve. If you avoid the discomfort of setting a firm boundary, then people walk all over you.

The Way Out
The way to guarantee you do yet another loop on the roundabout is to continue to squirm

away from those feelings and continue to try and avoid, escape or resist.

The way to stop the roundabout is to accept and embrace your experience—all of it!

The thing is, you actually don't have a choice. There is no real way to avoid what is true for you, or to avoid yourself. You can very temporarily pretend something else—but it always comes back, often with a vengeance. **Try to remind yourself, then, that acceptance is actually the easy way out.**

Avoidance creates divisions within you and puts some parts of you at war with other parts. While you are engaged in this exhausting battle, all your life's problems are exactly what they are, and will continue to be there until you take real action to solve them. So, why not just drop the exhausting battle and get to work on the problems as soon as possible?

Let's clear up a few misconceptions about "acceptance":

Accepting pain and discomfort doesn't mean you want it or that you're asking for it to continue. It only means that you are acknowledging reality as reality. Pain is inevitable, but suffering is not. What's the difference? A favorite Buddhist parable will explain:

If you are shot with a sharp dart, it will hurt. This "first dart" causes pain, no doubt about it.

But if we, for example, notice this pain and think "You shouldn't be such a weakling; it's only a small wound," then this thought is a "second dart." While the first dart causes pain, the second one causes (entirely optional) suffering. Many of us respond to natural and inevitable pains in life by trying to avoid them, judge them, analyze them—and in so doing we actually prolong them.

Acceptance, then, is to consciously choose not to add any more second darts. This means that we deal with the pain that really is there—the first dart—and we don't voluntarily make any more pain for ourselves than we need to! **Acceptance and avoidance are opposites.** The practice of acceptance is not to make you a passive doormat. Rather, it's to empower you. **The irony is that the quicker you can accept pain, the quicker you can move on from it!**

Avoidance can be a real stumbling block because it tends to amplify itself, creating the very problem that you are desperately trying to avoid. But even if you are trapped in an ongoing cycle of this kind, rest assured that there is always a way out. You can always, at any moment, respond differently. You can break that pattern and instill a new one—one that works for you rather than against you. "Sitting with" unpleasant realities is a way to make sure you're not giving them power over you.

One big caveat, however, is that acceptance is not the same as "positive thinking" or pretending that things are okay when they aren't. This is just—you guessed it—more avoidance. So saying, "Oh, it's no problem. There really isn't a dart stuck in my arm. I'm not in pain at all. I'm feeling great!" will just keep you trapped on the roundabout. Instead, try the following.

Step 1: Name your experience

See the roundabout you're trapped in and call it out. Is yours a tension, distraction, or intellectualizing loop? Do you have a habit of striving or numbing yourself out? If you've been avoiding discomfort for a long time, you might not even know what exactly you're experiencing, so take your time with this step.

Look at your life with the neutral eyes of a scientist or journalist and focus on "just the facts." That means no judgment, interpretation, or further avoidance. In other words, if you know you tend to be a perfectionist, don't immediately start judging yourself because perfectionism is a trait that makes you less perfect!

Simply take a step back and notice what is happening. At first, don't *do* anything about these observations—just become aware. If you can, try even saying this name out loud.

"Oh, I can tell I've fallen into my old rushing cycle again. I'm doing that thing where I rush and make mistakes, then rush to get away from those mistakes and make even more . . ."

"I'm avoiding this."

"I can tell I'm in second dart territory right now . . ."

Remember, however, that you're just naming, not name-calling! That means noticing without judging or interpreting. Say "I'm in my procrastination loop again" rather than "You've gone and done it again. You're stuck in your stupid cycle because you never learn. You're hopeless."

Step 2: Find a reason for getting off the roundabout

You already know how to get out of the roundabout—turn around and face your discomfort rather than flee from it. But in the heat of the moment, that's going to feel like an absolute impossibility! It's always going to be easier to stay on the loop than get out of it. It's always going to be hard to choose discomfort over comfort.

So, to make that decision, you need a very good reason. *Why* is it worth exiting the loop? Here are some potential reasons:

You get to save time you would have otherwise wasted going round and round.

You get to live a fuller, more engaged life on your own terms.

You get to grow and develop as a person.

So, for example, if you have named your experiential avoidance and recognize it as a pattern of giving up, look closely at what this behavior is costing you. Look at all the things you gain when you stop living that way. Maybe you realize that you would fulfill more of your potential if you stopped chickening out of things (not exactly non-judgmental language, but you get the picture!). Maybe you would feel more pride in yourself. Maybe you'd be able to be more vulnerable with people and create more intimacy with them. Maybe you'd speak up and stop letting others dominate.

Step 3: Make the decision

Your exit is discomfort. Choose it and you may find that, paradoxically, you instantly feel a bit better. The big thing you feared turns out not to be all that bad after all. You may realize that the only one who was giving it power was you. You may feel freer and more empowered when you realize that you actually *can* endure a little discomfort, and it's not the end of the world.

"Chosen pain" can help you transcend yourself. It can be a powerful steppingstone to the things you really want in life. When you truly grasp this, you may find yourself almost grateful when you encounter pain, because you know that on the other side of it might be something valuable! **Teach yourself to think less and wait less, and act more**. Don't give yourself too much time to dwell and come up with ways to avoid. Just act.

Summary:

- Laziness can be defined as the conscious unwillingness to put in the necessary effort required for a task, encompassing both mental and physical exertion. It's a cluster of behaviors, beliefs, attitudes, habits, and emotions, and acts as a trigger for secondary behaviors, thoughts, and feelings.

- Different types (or rather, causes) of laziness include confusion (I don't know what to do), fear (I can't do it), a fixed rather than growth mindset (I can't fail), fatigue (I'm too tired), apathy (I don't care), low self-belief (I'm just a lazy person; I can't do it), so-called "loss of heart" (What difference does it make, anyway?), and comfort orientation, or the preference for ease over effort (I'll do it . . . after I do this other fun thing).
- Your reason for procrastination (or mix of reasons) will determine what course of action you take to fix the problem. You may need more discipline, or to take a break, shift your mindset, reassess your goals, or work on time or energy management.
- The Shaolin monks have a similar model of "five hindrances to self-mastery," which include sensual desire, ill will, sloth and torpor, restlessness (distraction), and doubt/skepticism. Their overarching

solution for most laziness problems is not discipline, but self-mastery.

- You can remove the obstacles on your path using the RAIN method, which stands for recognize, accept, investigate, and non-identification. Become aware of your experience, accept it completely, inquire into its nature, and ensure you have some psychological distance so you can make conscious choices moving forward.

- What both models recognize is that *experiential avoidance* is at the heart of much laziness and procrastination. Adversity and discomfort are normal in life, but when we avoid them, we prolong our problems. Acceptance is the easy way out and entails not adding "second darts" to discomfort. The quicker you can accept pain, the quicker you can move on from it without turning it into suffering.

Chapter Two: The Discipline Mindset

In the previous chapter, we took a close look at exactly how we get in our own ways and undermine our attempts at growth, learning, and development. With a better understanding of what can go wrong, however, we're now better prepared to consider the healthier alternative. What does a disciplined person look like? How do they behave, think, feel?

If you've read any productivity self-help material before, or encountered any advice about self-discipline, you might have gotten the idea that it's just about what you DO. And in a way, this is one hundred percent true. **But what really matters is the mindset behind those actions.**

If you have heard that really effective and accomplished people wake up at 4 a.m. every morning, for example, you might then proceed to force yourself to do the same, hoping that it will make you similarly effective and accomplished. But this is to misunderstand that the behavior you can observe in someone is only the very end result of a long internal and completely private process.

Unless you understand those hidden motivations, mindsets, attitudes, and beliefs, then you are just blindly copying behavior without understanding what it means. The behavior is not what made that person successful—the mindset was. (This probably also explains why truly successful people don't tend to consume the kind of inspirational content that ends up being made about them!).

In this chapter we'll look at three things that characterize the mindset of people who end up displaying superior motivation, discipline, and effectiveness in life:

1. **Their ability to embrace and work with discomfort**
2. **Their psychological flexibility**
3. **Their capacity for emotional self-regulation**

Let's take a look at each in turn.

How to Embrace Discomfort

In the previous chapter, we saw that a big part of some people's "laziness" is the merry-go-round of experiential avoidance. However, even if you didn't particularly recognize yourself in those descriptions, almost all of us have a sub-optimal relationship with discomfort in a general sense, and it hinders our ability to reach our fullest potential.

Truly effective people are on more than speaking terms with discomfort—they have an ongoing long-term relationship with it! Their entire outlook in this area is counter to what is usually encouraged in conventional culture. We've already encountered the idea of "comfort orientation"—but what does "discomfort orientation" look like? The Stoics will be providing the theoretical backbone for this chapter since they knew the strength of the **connection between discomfort and growth**. But first, let's consider an example.

David has worked hard in his career and now has plenty of disposable income. Over time, he creates a "home entertainment system" that is more and more sophisticated. He buys bigger and bigger screens, invests in more expensive gaming equipment, and sinks himself regularly into a perfect sofa that feels like a cloud to sit on. There's a built-in drinks fridge and voice-controlled lighting.

At first, David saw this project as a kind of reward for earning well and a way to "relax" after work. But soon, he starts to become someone he isn't really proud of. He gains weight, he starts spending hours every day zoned out in front of the screen, and his relationships suffer. One day he has a full-scale temper tantrum ... because the batteries in his remote control need changing, and he resents having to get up off his seat. The ridiculous thing is, he doesn't even feel relaxed anymore. He just feels like an angry couch potato.

What happened? Some psychologists would say that David's problem is too much of a good thing. The term **"comfort creep" describes how new comforts increasingly become the norm for us so that we become numb to them and no longer appreciate or even recognize what used to provide satisfaction.** The substance we become addicted and desensitized to is actually comfort and pleasure itself. Sadly, modern life is packed to the brim with ways to constantly dial up comfort and convenience—a kind of "hedonistic numbing."

Our increasing comfort and reliance on modern conveniences have had detrimental effects on every area of life. As our comfort increases, our ability to tolerate uncertainty, our resilience to risk and failure, our creativity all decrease. The paradox is that **the easier we make our lives, the less able we are to tolerate things that are not easy.** The modern world has solved many of mankind's problems, but perhaps a little too well. Many of us have abundant access to food, information, pleasure, entertainment, medical care, and more without having to expend much effort. As a consequence:

We might get impatient and even angry when the internet goes down for literally thirty seconds.

We might feel violently aggrieved when someone disagrees with us or gets in our way.

We might resent having to go without pleasure even for a small amount of time.

We might get completely overwhelmed with even a little uncertainty or confusion.

We might become fragile and entitled, expecting life to provide certain conveniences, and being unable to cope when it doesn't.

The world is filled with messages to consume, relax, entertain yourself, and seek only pleasure and ease. But comfort can be a dangerous trap. To overcome the barriers created by "comfort creep," we need to do the exact opposite than what we're inclined to do: deliberately engage in activities that make us uncomfortable.

One such approach is the concept of misogi, adapted by Dr. Marcus Elliott from a Japanese Shinto practice. Misogi involves undertaking epic challenges in nature to reset the mind, body, and spirit and expand one's capabilities. Such "voluntary discomfort" served a few valuable functions:

1. Quieting and mastering the sensual appetites so they no longer dominate or get in the way of your life's goals
2. Cultivating real, experiential appreciation and gratitude for what you already have
3. "Vaccinating" yourself against future misfortunes by practicing how to manage them with grace and poise

right now, before that resilience is needed

4. Finally, to boost your sense of confidence in your ability to withstand adversity, and a deeper trust in your own mature willpower

As Seneca explains in the following quote, you are like a soldier who is making sure he is prepared for war while it is peace time:

> "Set aside a certain number of days, during which you shall be content with the scantiest and cheapest fare, with coarse and rough dress, saying to yourself the while: 'Is this the condition that I feared?' It is precisely in times of immunity from care that the soul should toughen itself beforehand for occasions of greater stress, and it is while Fortune is kind that it should fortify itself against her violence. In days of peace the soldier performs maneuvers, throws up earthworks with no enemy in sight, and wearies himself by gratuitous toil, in order that he may be equal to unavoidable toil. If you would not have a man flinch when the crisis comes, train him before it comes."—Seneca

A misogi is one way to ensure that you are "equal to unavoidable toil." **There are two rules: First, the task must be extremely difficult, with only around a fifty percent chance of success. Second, it must be relatively safe, ensuring personal well-being.** A misogi serves as a training exercise, but it is not about developing macho levels of fitness or physical prowess—*it's a mental challenge.*

The idea is to deliberately reach a point where you actually feel as though you cannot continue. It's at this point that the training really happens. By pushing through, by mustering courage and strength, by feeling discomfort and embracing it, allowing it to pass through and leave your will undisturbed, you are making enormous mental and emotional gains.

You experience firsthand proof that you may be underestimating yourself—not just in this exercise but in life in general. You learn what you are actually capable of if your fear and laziness are removed. You start to reflect on your habits, your choices, and the stories you tell about yourself. You start to become curious about the nature of your perceived limitations . . .

Embarking on a misogi is a psychological and spiritual task disguised as a physical challenge. Dr. Marcus Elliott wrote about his experience of a thirty-day hunting trip in the Alaskan wilderness, enduring harsh weather, scarcity of food, encounters with bears, long hikes in the snow, and extended periods of silence and boredom. The transformative effects of the misogi were evident upon his return, as he discovered increased mental and physical capabilities and a newfound ability to handle stress and challenges.

Again, however, **this is not a "toughening up" exercise for the physical body, but the mental, emotional, and spiritual body.** That means that a misogi can be almost any activity, so long as it follows the two rules outlined above. And though Elliot embarked on a month-long misogi challenge, you can recreate the same effects for yourself without such a long or dramatic commitment.

Introducing Discomfort into Your Life
Deliberately incorporating doses of discomfort into your daily life can have physical and mental benefits. Discomfort, when embraced with the right mindset, can expand your capabilities, fortify your resilience, and boost your confidence,

willpower, sense of purpose, integrity, creativity, and self-regulation. In fact, discomfort may be one of life's most abundant resources—if you know how to tap into it.

Here are some things to try:

Fasting

Hunger is not the end of the world. Not getting what you want when you want it is not the end of the world, either. In fact, occasionally embracing your hunger will teach you that having an appetite for something doesn't entitle you to satisfaction of that appetite, nor does it pose a serious threat. For most of us, hunger is occasional and not some awful emergency that needs to be quashed as quickly as possible. Basically, hunger is no big deal.

Sit with hunger for a moment and you may realize all sorts of interesting things. First, you may be surprised to learn that the sensation you're experiencing is not even hunger in the first place! Could it be boredom, sadness, anxiety, or just plain old greed? Are you just eating because of a completely mindless habit—for example, reaching for food because it's a certain time of day, or because you saw something on an ad or on TV?

Another thing that happens when you embrace and ride out hunger is that you teach yourself that you can actually pass through unpleasant sensations. Babies and children have no sense of proportion or self-discipline; when they feel upset, they react at once, as though their whole world is ending. Then their mood will flip again just as quickly. But as an adult, you can learn to see sensations, thoughts, desires, etc. as waves that will emerge but also subside again. One of the best feelings in the world is watching a craving appear and then watching as it fades again, and seeing yourself no longer care about what you were obsessed with just a few moments prior.

Think about what you can do with this capacity once strengthened! For example, a fasting practice may help you one day when you're online and just about to make an impulse purchase. You pause and look at this "hunger" for material things. You decide to consciously let that hunger go unmet for a while. Maybe you'll buy the thing tomorrow, if you still want it, but maybe you're okay with just leaving certain desires unsatisfied?

"Rucking" or Strenuous Physical Activity

Humans are uniquely designed to carry loads over long distances, which was essential for hunting and gathering in the past. Modern humans, on the other hand, experience few physical demands and are only minimally connected to their material environment.

A few connected problems may emerge: We may lose physical conditioning, gain weight, suffer poor posture from hunching in front of screens for hours on end, become self-absorbed, and start to believe that our only way of connecting to the world around us is abstractly. Our money is digital, we eat food wrapped in plastic that has followed supply chains that are invisible to us, and other people have built our houses. Our lifestyles may mean that entire days are lost to a purely symbolic realm; we are sedentary and lose a certain embodiment, our senses becoming dull.

One way to counter this is to drive in an SUV to an air-conditioned gym after work so a paid personal trainer can guide you in the use of various expensive machines. Another, more authentic way is simply to do what your ancestors did: carry a weighted backpack for long distances. You'll increase your cardiac fitness and muscle tone and improve bone density. You could drive, but become conscious of the things that are lost when you do.

The idea is to set up a direct connection between your physical effort and some observable results. Look back and see how far you've walked. Notice how you are able to carry increasingly heavy loads. Feel the ache in your muscles and understand that it is a direct result of you taking real action in the world. Practice this sort of activity often enough and you will find yourself feeling more grounded and purposeful.

For example, someone who regularly pushes themselves to camp on the weekends and carry heavy backpacks may discover that they are far more mentally tough at work. They notice that they are able to endure criticisms, delays, or difficulties with a much more robust attitude. There is a direct link, they realize, between this new attitude and their growing ability to put up with sore feet and keep walking no matter what!

Embracing Boredom

Have you ever hung around at a train station or in a restaurant on your own and immediately felt the urge to reach for your phone? Chances are, you had to experience a grueling twenty or thirty seconds without entertainment!

One of our most damaging cultural habits is the tendency to overvalue amusement and distraction. We may unconsciously believe that it is something close to a human right to never be bored—but is it? Our world has become so saturated with data that we have come to expect almost total and constant stimulation. We wake up and check our phones before we have even wiped the sleep from our eyes. We sit down to eat dinner and feel that the moment is boring unless we also simultaneously have a TV show to watch. We make sure that children have some kind of activity scheduled for every hour of every day, and when it's time to do chores or homework, we feel compelled to make this as interesting and entertaining for them as possible.

But if you had the privilege of growing up in a low-stimulus environment, you'll already know that boredom is a gift. Open space and silence give you time to process, rest, and generate your own ideas, rather than just consume other people's. Unplugging from constant distraction and noise actually enhances your own productivity and creativity in the long run. This is because the brain is forced into a more active and generative role rather than just sitting there and waiting to passively receive information from the outside.

This is why so many people experience "shower thoughts": profound or creative ideas and flashes of insight during a shower. For that brief moment in the shower, their brains are *not* being flooded with external information. Rather, it can contemplate things freely, making its own connections, coming to its own realizations, and generating its own theories, solutions, and questions.

To embrace boredom, simply make sure you're not always giving yourself something to do. If you're waiting in the doctor's office, just sit quietly rather than frantically looking for something to read. Give yourself twenty minutes every day where you just . . . do nothing. There's no need to try to turn it into some effortful meditation exercise, either. Just imagine turning the engine off in your brain and stopping for a while. You will develop patience, serenity, and better self-regulation if you are perfectly comfortable to just be who you are, in the moment as it is, without distraction.

Some other exercises you can try to make conscious use of discomfort are:

- **"Temporary poverty"**—spend a period of time consuming very little. Go without. That may mean dressing very humbly, eating little, or repairing something old rather than buying new. It's not about punishment, and it's not a competition. Rather, it's about learning to master your own sensual desires, your fears, and your strengths.

- **Choose uncomfortable situations where a comfortable one would be easy and convenient.** For example, take a cold or very short shower. Wear clothes that leave you feeling a little cold. Sleep on the floor or force yourself to walk somewhere even though you have a car.

- **Forego a pleasure that you might have been taking for granted.** Decide not to drink, have a candy bar, or sleep in on the weekend.

- **Do things yourself.** Wash your laundry by hand, write your notes out with pen and paper rather than on a PC, cook from scratch, or figure out how to fix something without help.

While you do all these things, remember not to become a martyr or get distracted by how miserable you are—that's not the point. Rather, ask if the discomfort you're experiencing is as bad as you thought. Ask if discomfort, even if it is great, truly stops you from doing what you need and want to do. Finally, pay attention to the fact that you *can* endure it, even learn from it. What else can you apply these lessons to?

Develop Psychological Flexibility Using ACT

During the Covid-19 pandemic, many people found themselves experiencing mental distress they did not think they were capable of. There were those who were surprised to find themselves anxious, depressed, and feeling totally fragile. Despite being mature, capable people with life skills that had served them well, they were soon feeling emotionally unregulated, reactive, and unable to connect properly with others.

Naturally, the pandemic was a complicated phenomenon, and no two people experienced it in the same way. However, it's worth looking back to try to understand *why* some people were better able to cope with those unavoidable stressors while others floundered. One big factor may be **psychological flexibility, which is the ability to continually take action in accordance with one's values, despite change, uncertainty, and distress.**

Psychological inflexibility, then, is the **in**ability to act this way, especially when faced with an extremely challenging or unexpected situation. When we are psychologically inflexible, we may have a knee-jerk response to avoid discomfort and rely on avoidance as our main coping strategy. We may be stuck in a passive-reactive mode, rather than consciously looking to the future and choosing our actions based on our principles and goals.

Psychological flexibility forms, along with the ability to discomfort tolerance and self-regulation, a trio of attitudes that form the bedrock of a disciplined life. In the last section we explored how the inability to tolerate pain, discomfort, boredom, or even things like uncertainty can lower our resilience and self-confidence in the long term, even though we may believe that the easy, pleasurable life is what we really want. In the same way, psychological inflexibility seems like a good strategy in the moment, but in the long run is an approach that undermines your overall well-being.

Let's imagine a simple example in the hypothetical life of someone living through the early days of the Covid-19 pandemic. Jenny's elderly mother is in a care home on the other side of the country, and when the whole area is put into lockdown, Jenny is immediately alarmed that she can no longer do her twice monthly visits. Let's consider two attitudes she can take to these circumstances that are out of her control.

Attitude 1, psychological inflexibility: "I can't believe this is happening; this is awful. I could just cry. What if something terrible happens and I can't be there for her? I can't bear it and it's not fair. She may die in the next few years, and then what? Is this the last opportunity to spend time with her? I just don't know what I'm going to do. It's awful. I can't do this. If I had known this was going to happen, I would have spent so much more time with her back in the day . . ."

Attitude 2, psychological flexibility: "I can't believe this is happening. It's really awful, and I feel so bad about it. But I absolutely refuse to let this get in the way of staying in touch with the people I care about it. If I can't visit my mother, then I'll phone her or get her on a video call. I'll chat with the nurses, and we can organize something. I don't know how I'll do it yet, but I'll figure something out. She needs me now. She's my mother, and I'm going to be there for her one way or another."

You can immediately see the difference. Let's look at the second response and break down exactly why it's different from the first:

Attitude 1 is fixated on a scary possible future and regrets from the past; attitude 2 is focused on the present and what can be done here and now.

Attitude 1 faces negative feelings with avoidance and resistance ("I can't do it. I can't bear it."), while attitude 2 acknowledges the feelings but isn't *fused* with them entirely; they do not get in the way of meaningful action.

Attitude 2 is active, and that action is driven by clearly identified goals (family is very important), while attitude 1 is reactive and disempowered.

Finally, notice how in attitude 2, Jenny is actually able to consider things from her mother's point of view and is telling herself a story that guides her to positive solutions-focused thinking. The irony is that in attitude 1, the relentless focus on the unfairness of it all actually would keep Jenny trapped in those passive, resentful feelings. Jenny can be a victim, or she can be a conscious, active agent in her own life.

From this example you can probably see the value in shifting from the first kind of attitude to the second. This means moving from:

- Experiential avoidance to willingness to experience
- Fusion to defusion (i.e., to non-identification with sensations)
- Past/future focus to present-moment awareness
- Rigid stories about experiences to flexible perspective-taking
- Lack of direction to clear values and principles
- Inaction to committed, value-driven action

From this perspective, **our main goal is to continuously move closer to the things in life that are important to us.** Trying to avoid pain and discomfort or escape difficult experiences is one of the main ways we lose focus on those important things—**we put our attention on avoiding the difficulty rather than on moving forward to what we value and want for ourselves.**

You could try to reframe your thoughts (as is done in CBT—cognitive behavioral therapy), or you could explore things in the past that created the present problem (as is sometimes done in psychotherapy), but there is an approach that sees difficulty and **negative experiences as a problem only insomuch as they interfere with your values-driven, meaningful life in the present**. This model is called ACT—Action and Commitment Therapy.

Simply, ACT is about learning to stay focused on what you value no matter what negative or uncomfortable sensations arise—this ability is what is termed psychological flexibility. When we are focused on our suffering and how to avoid it, our perception becomes narrow, fixed, and brittle. But when we stay in the moment and behave as values-driven active agents, we become more flexible and adaptive. Life starts to look very different!

How can this idea of psychological flexibility in ACT help us with our own procrastination demons?

ACT encourages openness to all thoughts and emotions, regardless of their nature. This means accepting *both* positive and negative thoughts and feelings, without judgment or the need to escape or avoid. When it comes to tasks you don't really want to do, you can choose to stay present and fully engage with the activity, rather than being consumed by negative thoughts or avoiding the task altogether. By accepting and acknowledging any discomfort or unpleasant emotions that may arise, individuals can still take action in line with their values, even if they don't particularly enjoy the task at hand.

This can be a breakthrough idea for some people: *You do not have to like a task to do it.* And you can experience unpleasant emotions around that task without those emotions meaning anything in particular. You are always empowered to act toward your goals and in line with your values, whatever passing sensations you are experiencing. This can be an extraordinary freedom—you can act just because you choose to! Motivation, inspiration, ease, excitement, pleasure . . . none of these things are actually necessary.

To develop psychological flexibility in your own life, here are six mindset shifts that will increase your psychological flexibility:

Acceptance

Develop willingness by practicing mindfulness and opening up to difficult thoughts and feelings. Engage in formal mindfulness practice by sitting in silence and just allowing these experiences to be present. Informally, stop trying to avoid or eliminate painful thoughts and feelings, and instead, embrace them as part of the journey toward what you truly care about.

To identify areas of avoidance in your life, ask yourself, **"What am I unwilling to feel?" Use this question as a guide to focus your work.** Instead of avoiding that sensation, see if you can just accept it for what it is. The more you practice opening up to discomfort and facing it head-on, the better you'll be able to stay connected to your values and goals rather than getting caught in avoidance.

For example, Jenny notices she is feeling panicked and fearful. She notices the thought "I could just cry." She **allows herself** to fully acknowledge these feelings of sadness and hopelessness, simply because they are part of reality. But she doesn't add "second darts" to this reality. She doesn't try to avoid those feelings by pretending they aren't happening, or numb them out with distractions or substances. She doesn't judge or diagnose these feelings or feel guilt or shame about them. She doesn't embrace them, either, or exaggerate her sadness until she's in utter despair. She just pauses within herself and becomes aware. "I am sad right now. It's a feeling I'm having." And that's all.

Acceptance is the first step. We then need to learn to move from fusion (being entangled with thoughts) to defusion (seeing thoughts as separate from yourself).

Cognitive Defusion

Your thoughts are events happening inside your awareness. They are not absolute reality.

Recognize that thoughts are simply thoughts, not definitive truths. This will allow you to gain a little psychological distance and realize that sensations and experiences do pass. Your thoughts and feelings don't define who you are. And they do not go on forever.

If you're ever feeling trapped in a spiral of negative thinking, try this quick exercise: Raise your hand in the air, wave it back and forth, and simultaneously say aloud, "I'm not waving my hand back and forth." See? Instant proof that just because your mind thinks something, it doesn't mean it's automatically true!

Once you truly grasp this, you then empower yourself to *choose* thoughts that are more helpful and aligned with your goals. Let's say that Jenny accepts her feelings of sadness about her situation. She becomes aware and notices a few thoughts and beliefs that emerge in her. One thought is: "I'm a victim; other people are controlling my life." This thought, she notices, influences her behavior. In fact, it's a big part of what makes her feel sad, and it also causes her to want to escape the situation and avoid it entirely ("I can't bear it"). If you genuinely thought you had no control and that other people's actions were the only determiner of your reality, you'd be upset, too! And worse, you'd feel that there was no point in acting.

When Jenny sees this, she realizes that this way of thinking is actively undermining the things she cares about (family) and making her feel worse. She can only see this, though, once she loosens her grip on her perception and realizes she can have a different, more useful one.

Present Moment Contact

This one is easy and can be done, should be done, literally at any time: Intentionally bring your attention back to the present whenever you find yourself preoccupied with thoughts about the past or future.

To practice present moment contact, take a moment to focus on the stimuli coming in through your five senses. Your body is always located in the real world, in the present. Fully inhabit your body, and you automatically inhabit the present moment. The great thing about the present moment is that not only is it far more manageable to engage with, but it also happens to be the only place from which you can *actually* change your world—no matter how much you regret the past or ruminate on the future, the only place you can genuinely act is in the here and now. So you might as well stay there!

Pause wherever you are and direct your attention to physical sensations, sounds, smells, sights, and tastes. This helps ground you in the present moment and shift your focus away from past or future-oriented thinking. In Jenny's example, she could notice herself getting upset and choose instead to focus on the fact that in the here and now, her life is just fine. Though her head is going a million miles an hour, she focuses on the fact that her body is actually safe, warm, and comfortable. There is a beautiful sunset outside. The cat is sleeping in the corner, and she can smell dinner cooking in the next room. She is breathing, awake, aware, and alive. When she realizes the room she's in, the moment she's inhabiting, everything instantly feels like so much less of a problem.

Remember that thoughts about the past or future are not reality; they are just cognitive events happening in the present. By recognizing this, you can stay connected to the joy, meaning, and opportunities available in your life *right now*, rather than being driven by thoughts and feelings about other times and places. You become more flexible, more alive, and far more capable.

Self-as-Context

Practice flexible perspective-taking by recognizing that rigid stories about ourselves and others are not the whole truth. Challenge the tendency to flatten individuals into two-dimensional caricatures and instead see them as complex, multi-faceted human beings with strengths, flaws, hopes, and fears. **Try to put yourself in their shoes and explore their perspective, fostering empathy and understanding.**

Jenny might be telling herself a stressful story about how she is a bad daughter who has abandoned her mother in a care home, about how her mother is all alone on death's door and it's Jenny's fault . . . but that's just a story Jenny is telling herself. It may be that Jenny's mother is not in the least concerned about the lockdown, or even that she found Jenny's visits unnecessary and is happy to talk over the phone instead.

Furthermore, develop a sense of a flexible self by understanding that no label or story can fully capture the complexity of a human life, yours or another person's. Recognize that your self-worth is not solely determined by external achievements or comparisons to others. Embrace the idea that your experiences and personal growth, even in the face of challenges, contribute to your development as a person.

Values
Move toward values by reconnecting your day-to-day activities to what truly matters to you. Start by clarifying your values—those

ways of being and doing that are intrinsically meaningful to you. Reflect on how you want to be remembered and what qualities you want to embody throughout your life.

Jenny does *not* value feeling like a shameful guilty failure or a victim, so why should she spend all her mental energy on being one, or else fighting against being one? Instead, she could pour her attention and will into what she *does* want to be: a loving, loyal, and devoted person who prioritizes family connections.

Try the tombstone exercise to gain that crystal clarity that comes from focusing on what matters . . . and ignoring all the noise that doesn't. You do the exercise by simply imagining what you would want your tombstone or obituary to say at the end of your life. Perhaps compare it to what it would say if you died today. "Jenny was a guilty and anxious person"? "Jenny was a victim"? Realize that the difference between the two comes from focused, values-driven action. Choose not to let fleeting experiences and obstacles define you.

Remember that values are different from goals. Goals are specific achievements that exist in the past or future, while values represent ongoing qualities that guide your actions in the present. Values give meaning to your actions and persist throughout your life, adapting and finding new expressions as circumstances change.

Committed Action

This is where ACT really starts to shine. The best way out of any predicament is to take inspired, meaningful action in your life, no matter how small. In Jenny's case, she might choose to immediately reach out to her mother and start planning a call so she can maintain that valuable family connection despite the new obstacle.

This does two things—it solves her immediate problem, but it also reinforces Jenny's conception of herself as an active agent who is in control of her life. After acting, she instantly feels less anxious because she knows she has taken responsibility for steering her life, rather than passively waiting for life to happen to her. She feels less anxious because she feels more in control. And because this action is aligned with her goals, it is meaningful and brings a sense of commitment and resilience. We can imagine the stress and adversity of life as a rough sea, but we have committed, value-driven action to guide us like a compass. We chart our way *through* the unpleasant situations rather than getting trapped in them. We create paths to our sense of reward despite obstacles in our path.

Committed action is essential for meaningful change. It involves aligning behaviors with values and taking small steps in new directions. **To support committed action, you can utilize strategies like reminders, records, rewards, routines, relationships, reflecting, and restructuring.**

Behavior change can be challenging, so these strategies provide scaffolding until the new behaviors become self-reinforcing. The ultimate goal is for the new behavior to be intrinsically rewarding and continue naturally.

Consider a final, very mundane example: You have a report to compile for work, but it's boring and you're procrastinating. So, you truthfully acknowledge you find it boring, without resistance or judgment (acceptance); you remind yourself that your boredom is just a fleeting experience you're having, not your whole world (defusion); and you consciously choose not to escape into mindless internet scrolling (present moment contact) and instead remind yourself both that people are depending on you for this report and that you derive satisfaction out of being the one that can help them in this way (self-as-context and values).

You then take committed action—not because you magically don't find the task boring anymore, but because you realize you can find it boring and act anyway. After a few minutes on the task, you forget why you were so resistant in the first place, you complete the report, you feel good about yourself. You have just taught yourself a lesson: You are in control. *You* determine the outcome of your life.

The Ninety-Second Rule of Emotional Control

"When we can no longer change a situation, we are challenged to change ourselves . . . Everything can be taken from a human but one thing: the last of the human freedoms—to choose one's attitude in any given set of circumstances, to choose one's own way."

—Viktor Frankl, *Man's Search for Meaning*

Emotional control is a simple concept that is nevertheless not easy: It is the ability to **choose our response to a situation rather than allowing that situation to determine the choice you make.** You may recognize that this is essentially what the ACT technique described above teaches you: At the end of the day, we have a "human freedom" to respond as we choose. Even if we are emotionally overwhelmed. Even if the situation we are in is unfair, unpleasant, painful, scary, or confusing.

Emotional control doesn't mean we become emotionless or that we don't care about anything. It means we have all the emotions we ordinarily would, but they occupy a different place in our world. When we have emotional control, it's as though our fleeting experiences are passengers in a car we are driving, rather than being the driver of that car themselves.

Elsewhere Frankl has said, "Between stimulus and response there is a space. In that space is our power to choose our response. In our response lies our growth and our freedom." But often in life we have zero control over what our circumstances are, **or** over our knee-jerk reactions and responses to those. For example, someone stands on our toe and we immediately cry out in pain. We are told bad news and are instantly in shock and disbelief. None of this is under our control—including the emotion of anger, pain, or fear.

So, perhaps the term "emotional control" is misleading, because in fact, we don't need to control anything. The gap or space that Frankl is talking about can also be understood as the short period of time in which we feel an automatic emotional response to something— before it's over. After that, everything is under our control again. In other words, it's what we choose to do next that makes all the difference.

Neuroscientist and author of *My Stroke of Insight*, Jill Bolte Taylor, explains what she thinks of as a **ninety-second rule: "When a person has a reaction to something in their environment, there's a ninety-second chemical process that happens; any remaining emotional response is just the person choosing to stay in that emotional loop."**

> "Essentially, when you look at cells in the circuitry of the brain, every reactivity is simply a group of cells performing their function. From the moment you have the thought that

there's a threat and that circuit of fear gets triggered, it will stimulate the emotional circuitry related to it, which is the fight-or-flight reaction. That will trigger a physiological dumpage of usually norepinephrine or anger into the bloodstream. It will flush through you and flush out of you in less than 90 seconds. So from the moment you think the thought that triggers that whole cascade of events to the chemical flushing out of you takes less than 90 seconds.

[. . .] Look at the second hand on a watch. As soon as you look at it, you're now observing yourself having this physiological response instead of engaging with it. It will take less than 90 seconds, and you will feel better. Of course, you can always go back to thinking those thoughts that restimulate the loop. There's probably a thought somewhere in your brain of somebody who did you wrong 20 years ago. Every time you think of that person it still starts that circuit. When things are getting hot and you're getting hot-headed, look at your watch. It takes 90 seconds to dissipate that anger response."

Knowing that these kinds of experiences are short-lived makes it easier to accept them, defuse from them, and remind yourself of what really matters—your values and goals as described by ACT. It's a little like realizing that even the strongest and most unpleasant experience will only max out at around ninety seconds. Doesn't it make sense to ensure that it only lasts ninety seconds, and that you don't necessarily drag it out for longer than that?

After ninety seconds, the initial chemical reaction is over. If you *still* feel fear, anger, anxiety, or any other emotion, it's not your physiology that's fueling it—it's your own thoughts re-stimulating the chemical changes. **It's your choice to keep refreshing that ninety seconds again and again**. These thoughts construct a feedback loop that re-activate the chemical response and embed the emotion deeper.

The irony is that our uniquely human ability to think makes it possible for us to get stuck in the emotional loop. So, you feel anger that you have to do more work than you first thought. This anger lasts just ninety seconds. But then you find yourself getting angry about the anger. Then you're feeling guilty about that secondary anger. Then you're finding additional things to be mad about, and before you know it, you're caught in an awful reinforcing loop—only the first ninety seconds of it were unavoidable, and the rest was purely optional!

Four Strategies to Work with the Ninety-Second Window

When we have control over our emotions, we are less likely to be swayed by impulse, allowing us to stay focused on our long-term goals and commitments. We give ourselves the power to make conscious decisions for more intentional living. The awareness of being able to recognize triggers, develop self-awareness, and regulate emotional responses helps you embrace personal responsibility and self-discipline. One obvious benefit of mastering this kind of self-control: We just enjoy our lives more and deliberately opt to not make things harder than they need to be.

Just knowing about the ninety-second rule gives you an advantage: Promise yourself that you will not make any decisions inside this period. Just ride things out and then take action afterward, when you'll likely feel clearer. Acting when you're in the full flush of emotion may mean you create bigger problems for yourself. Just pause, notice, detach, and you'll be amazed at how quickly the "wave" comes and goes again.

1. Get to know your red flags

To cultivate self-discipline, it is essential to familiarize yourself with your own red flags. Take the time to explore and identify the specific triggers that activate negative emotional responses within you even before the ninety-second window begins. For example, when you put off something, it is maybe because you love to procrastinate or you just love being in your comfort zone. It could also be because you lack structure or find everything uninspiring.

Reflect on the individuals, situations, timings, environments, or even specific stimuli like music that tend to provoke these reactions. By gaining a deeper understanding of your triggers, you can start taking ownership of them.

Example: You're in a study session, when suddenly you encounter a difficult passage in a textbook. Within a matter of seconds, you are caught in a familiar old loop: You feel stupid and inadequate because you don't immediately understand what you're reading, and then this feeling makes you want to escape. You recognize that this is a trigger— and it usually has you immediately getting up off your seat and rummaging in the kitchen for a soothing snack to make you feel better.

Knowing that the thought "I'm stupid" and the feeling of confusion is a trigger for you, you can consciously choose to ride it out for ninety seconds rather than allow it to send you to the kitchen. Perhaps you do a quick grounding exercise, run through an affirmation ("it's okay not to understand things the first time round. I'm learning. I'm improving"), and then after a minute or two, that feeling isn't so pronounced anymore. You push on. Congratulations—you avoided an hours-long procrastination loop.

2. Identify an emotional reaction

In the realm of self-discipline, it is crucial to understand that every emotion manifests in a distinct physiological "signature" as various bodily systems are activated, including the cardiovascular, skeletomuscular, neuroendocrine, and autonomic nervous systems. Take intentional pauses to observe and recognize these bodily reactions when experiencing different emotions.

For instance, anger may be accompanied by a clenched jaw, tense muscles, and an increased or rapid heartbeat, while happiness often brings about a sense of inner lightness, relaxed muscles, and regular breathing patterns.

To enhance self-discipline, regularly tune into your body and cultivate body awareness. When you find yourself overwhelmed by an emotion, take a moment to inquire "What do I feel in my body?" or "What am I noticing physically?" Approach these questions with a sense of curiosity, exploring the physical sensations associated with your emotional state.

Example: You're in your study session and start to notice your interest and attention flagging. You suddenly start feeling really uninspired by the content. You pause and do a body scan. You notice sore eyes, a heavy feeling all over, tension in the forehead, tight shoulders. You realize that you are not losing interest in the work or being lazy—you're just tired! You take a break and return refreshed.

3. Label the emotion

Developing an extensive emotional vocabulary can greatly support your journey. The ability to name and identify specific emotions provides a powerful tool for understanding and managing them effectively. As in the last point, there's great value in knowing the difference between "tired" and "unmotivated" because the solution to each problem will be very different.

Often, people will self-castigate by diagnosing every negative feeling in themselves the same way. They may uniformly consider themselves lazy or stupid or unmotivated, when in reality they are experiencing a range of complex emotional responses, some of them completely valid and appropriate.

Instead of relying on broad descriptions like "I'm being lazy," expand your emotional vocabulary to include more nuanced distinctions and a deeper understanding of your inner experiences. Incidentally, mislabeling is often just judgment in disguise, so being more accurate and neutral with labeling your feelings tends to make self-compassion easier.

Example: At work, you notice yourself responding negatively to a task. You assume that not wanting to do the task means you feel "unmotivated" or "bored" by it. But when you really pay attention, you discover that this is actually just an assumption you've made.

Exploring your feelings without any judgment reveals that you are actually feeling *overwhelmed*.

It's not that the task is boring; it's that you have no idea where to begin with it and feel exhausted and burnt out just thinking about it! Many people mislabel excitement as fear, or disinterest with anger. When you remove any ideas about what you feel you "should" be experiencing, you may be surprised at what you are actually experiencing.

4. Acceptance

Maintaining emotional control does not imply repression of our feelings. Our emotions play a crucial role in healthy adaptation and contribute to an emotionally fulfilling life. Therefore, it's important to allow feelings to naturally arise and subside without judgment or attempts to alter them. Instead, adopt a mindset of curiosity and become an observer of your emotions. Take charge and exercise control when you recognize that certain emotions should not overpower you.

Example: You are embarking on a new training course and finding it extremely difficult to get through the assignments, somehow always procrastinating. You and everyone around you may be telling you a story that goes: "The course is difficult but very much worth it; you have to push though, so be dedicated. We know you can do it!"

But this may be hiding your real emotions. You may be unable to do the course because it doesn't actually align with your values, and every time you sit down to work on it, you're reminded of something you're trying to avoid: the fact that you are long overdue a career change. This is an inconvenient side of procrastination that often goes unacknowledged: Sometimes, you can't do something because on some level you know it's not what you want to be doing. Acceptance is the only way to know what you're working with and the only thing that will tell you whether you do in fact need to "push through" . . . or completely reconsider your career path.

Summary:

- Actions matter, but what's important is the attitude and mindset behind those actions.
- Three things characterize the mindsets of people with motivation, discipline, and effectiveness in life: the ability to embrace

and work with discomfort, psychological flexibility, and a capacity for emotional self-regulation.

- There is an unavoidable connection between discomfort and growth, so growth requires getting familiar with discomfort. Comfort creep explains that the easier we make our lives, the less able we are to tolerate things that are not easy. One solution is to deliberately introduce and embrace discomfort in your life—for example, with cold showers, hard physical activity, or embracing boredom.

- Psychological flexibility is the ability to continually take action in accordance with one's values, despite change, uncertainty, and distress. It can be cultivated using the ACT approach, where you stay focused on what you value no matter what negative or uncomfortable sensations arise.

- ACT skills include accepting all emotional responses, defusing and detaching from that experience, remaining anchored in the present, staying connected to your values, perspective switching, and choosing committed action on your own terms.

- The ninety-second rule of emotional control teaches us that "when a person has a reaction to something in their environment, there's a ninety-second chemical process that happens; any remaining emotional response is just the person choosing to stay in that emotional loop." Knowing this, we can choose our response beyond the ninety seconds. Get to know your triggers, label your emotions as they arise, and accept them.

Chapter Three: The Discipline Habit

Discomfort tolerance.
Psychological flexibility.
Emotional regulation.

If you can master these three mindsets in your own life, you can start to appreciate the secret that every truly effective person knows: **It's possible to harness your mind power and use it to work for you, rather than constantly be at its mercy or even have it work against you.**

What's remarkable is that this possibility is available to anyone no matter where they currently are in their lives. No matter what happens today, you can wake up tomorrow and choose to use your mind as a tool to help you build the life you want for yourself. No matter what is happening right now, you can choose what your experience will be and how you will act.

Now that we've taken a good look at what it's like to *not* have self-discipline, as well as the three key ingredients for the discipline mindset, let's dive into the problem that likely brought you to this book in the first place: procrastination. We are now going to put that mindset to use and manifest it in *consistent, real-world action*—that is, in habit.

The Procrastination Doom Loop

Two things seem true about procrastination: Everyone has a theory about how not to do it, yet everyone seems to do it!

According to Derek Thompson's article in *The Atlantic*, procrastination is related more to a person's emotions rather than their time management skills. Breaking the habit of procrastination is therefore a psychological exercise rather than simply a matter of being more organized. The insight here is that self-discipline is NOT about having a well-structured schedule, for example, or a good morning routine. Rather, it's about maintaining the kind of mindset that would make those habits and behaviors possible.

Joseph Ferrari, a psychology professor at DePaul University, compares telling a chronic procrastinator to *just do it* to telling a clinically depressed person to cheer up. Through his research, Ferrari has identified two main reasons behind procrastination:

- **People delay taking action because they don't feel like they are in the right mood to complete the task.**
- **People believe that their mood will change in the near future.**

Here, you'll probably recognize a few of the elements we've already discussed, namely experiential avoidance, comfort orientation, a fixed mindset, and the failure to accept the present moment and everything that is true for you in that moment.

Ferrari refers to the above two factors as the "procrastination doom loop." You can probably guess how the loop goes:

1. You put off an important task
2. You feel guilt, shame, or anxiety
3. These anxious emotions then make it even less likely you'll muster the

emotional and cognitive energy needed to complete the task (because remember, you believe you have to be in the right mood to start)
4. You keep on putting off the task
5. You feel even more guilt, shame, and anxiety
6. . . . and so on for a few cycles, and then
7. DOOM

Very quickly you find yourself in a nasty loop. There are many interesting theories about what starts us out on a procrastination loop, but in a way this is not as important as figuring out why the loop is maintained. In other words—**a vicious cycle has no root**!

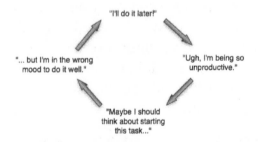

"I'll do it later!"

"... but I'm in the wrong mood to do it well."

"Ugh, I'm being so unproductive."

"Maybe I should think about starting this task..."

Procrastination is far more complex than commonly believed. It is amplified and driven by negative emotions, or rather our response to them, and is not simply a result of poor time management or laziness. Recognizing the influence of these emotions is crucial for tackling procrastination effectively.

Neil Fiore is author of *The Now Habit* and has offered three of the reasons he believes people procrastinate:

Perfectionism: Setting unrealistically high standards for ourselves, often influenced by external sources, makes it difficult to start working. The fear of failure and negative self-talk further intensifies anxiety and contributes to procrastination (you'll recognize this as a part of a fixed mindset, i.e., the all-or-nothing thinking that tells us that we either do it perfectly or we fail . . . and we absolutely cannot fail. The only possible option given these conditions? Don't do anything).

Fear of success: Procrastination can also result from a fear of achieving success. Concerns about potential social alienation, significant life changes, and increased expectations from others can create anxiety and lead to avoidance of work. If we do well, does that mean the demands on us are instantly going to be increased? That's definitely a reason not to do well!

Frustration and powerlessness: Procrastination may be a way of exerting control over a situation where one feels powerless. It can also be a response to internalized beliefs that working hard only leads to more work, leading to a desire to escape through procrastination.

University of Durham's Professor Fuchsia Sirois also believes that procrastination is about better mod management and not just time management:

> "At its core, procrastination is about not being able to manage your moods and emotions. Although many think impulsivity and self-control are the problems—and they do play a factor—underneath is a poor emotional response."

Sirois also explains how poor temporal thinking is to blame. Essentially, we have the tendency to imagine that our future selves will be very different from our current selves—in fact research done with MRI scans show that the parts of our brains activated by thinking of ourselves in the future are the same parts that activate when we think of a stranger! Sirois says,

"This is important as if you perceive your future self this way then it's easier to do something that might harm that person, leaving them a huge task rather than doing it yourself now. [. . .] As your future self might feel psychologically distant to you now, you might also see them as a kind of superhero. You might say 'Future me will have all the ideas because they'll be well-rested' or 'Future me won't have writer's block.' However, the truth is that we really don't change much in a short period of time."

So, who is right, Fiore, Ferrari, or Sirois? You're probably beginning to notice that *all* theories of procrastination are variations on a theme. The exact way it plays out in your unique life may be hard to predict, but you can probably identify the same mechanisms outlined here. Perhaps the procrastination looks like this:

You have a task to do (file a tax return). You build this task up in your mind so that there is already a lot of fear, fatigue, and resistance associated with it before you even begin ("ill will"). You see this task up ahead of you and make a decision that because this task is so big and important, you have to do it properly (remember how you messed up last year's tax return?). You conclude that anything other than perfection this time round counts as a catastrophe, and you gear yourself up to pushing through this monumentally difficult task.

You sit down to do this task you've spent hours convincing yourself is going to be hell on earth. And, big surprise, you don't much feel in the mood for hell on earth. You're nowhere near energetic and focused enough to do so important a task. It's a tax return! You can't make a mistake! In fact, while you're thinking about mistakes, just imagine what it would be like if you did it wrong and then were audited or worse, fined. Or even worse, went to jail for tax fraud . . .

You feel so bad that you literally cannot function. Your mind is a blur, and you decide the whole plan has gone wrong. You're too tired. You're too stressed. You can do it tomorrow—because tomorrow you won't be as tired and as stressed as you are now, right? A tax return will only take you an hour to do, and you definitely have an hour tomorrow.

Tomorrow comes around, you sit down to do the tax return, and you find you are still not in the "right mood"—in fact everything is worse now because it's still not done and you're one day closer to the deadline. Round and round you go until you get to the final step, the DOOM part, where you're up late at night on the day of the deadline, completing your tax return. You've just taught yourself that this activity is a big, monumental ordeal, and you'll remember this night the same time next year . . .

As you can see, the above example contains a little of all the theories we've explored so far.

But what can we do to stop the loop once and for all?

Remember that although procrastination can feel complex, there are many, many ways to stop yourself and get off the merry-go-round:

Practice Self-Compassion

Procrastinators, especially chronic procrastinators, tend to be hard on themselves both before and after completing a task. Step back from self-criticism and acknowledge that everyone makes mistakes and experiences procrastination. **Forgive yourself for making a small mistake rather than chaining yourself to a loop that will result in even bigger mistakes.**

Recognize that procrastination is a common human experience and not the end of the world. Be kind to yourself and move forward with the task instead of getting stuck in a cycle of self-judgment. This is where acceptance comes in. So, you feel bad. That's fine. But don't allow this feeling to feed back into the loop and convince you that you cannot act.

Reframe Your Thoughts

Change your perspective and reorient yourself toward your goals and values, not your negative feelings (as in ACT). Instead of viewing the task negatively or as a burden, reframe it as something meaningful and valuable—or something that brings you closer to something meaningful and valuable. Reframe how you think of success, failure, and perfection. Rename failure as learning, for example, perfectionism as avoidance, and difficult challenges as nothing more than games or fun puzzles.

Ask yourself:

- How will completing this goal be valuable in how I see myself?
- How will completing this goal be valuable in how others see me?
- How will completing this goal be valuable to my personal growth?

Take Baby Steps

Commit to action in the present, even if it's tiny and even if you are not in the right mood.

The trick is that the only way you really will be a different person in the future is if you take concrete action *now* to make that a reality. Don't bank on being in a magically better frame of mind in the future. Instead, take however you feel (afraid, bored, lazy, etc.) and assume it's a given. Assume you will always feel that way. Where does that leave you? Well, it means you have to just get on with acting.

But you can be easy on yourself—your action does not have to be enormous. It just has to be big enough to move you out of the inertia of procrastination. Repeatedly teach yourself that you can act independent of your mood. The secret is that *motivation does not lead to action; instead it's the other way around—when you take action, you gradually build up motivation.* If you've flatlined on your motivation levels, don't sit around and wait for someone to come and make you do what you need to do. Rather, act even though you don't quite feel it, then notice that after you do, you feel a tiny bit more inspired. Then take the next step. Then the next.

Finding Your Flashlight

According to Amisha Jha, author of *Peak Mind: Find Your Focus, Own Your Attention, Invest 12 Minutes a Day*, our attention operates in three major modes:

1. **Flashlight (orienting system)**
2. **Caution sign (alerting system)**
3. **Juggler (executive functioning)**

Flashlight: Our attention acts like a flashlight, gathering information about whatever it's focused on. It can be directed externally to visual, auditory, or olfactory cues, as well as internally to thoughts, experiences, and memories. It functions in much the same way as a flashlight beam does when beamed into the darkness—it helps us selectively place awareness on just one aspect of reality at a time.

The strength and focus of our attentional flashlight impact our perception, biases, judgments, actions, effectiveness, and overall happiness. It's important to have control over the beam of our attention to avoid getting stuck on negative thoughts. This may help us understand, for example, why the ACT technique works—we shift our flashlight beam from our negative feelings (or avoiding them) onto our values and goals. Likewise, if we are trying to master sensual desire like the Shaolin monks suggest, we need to pull our attention away from temporary pleasures in the present and onto their effects in the future.

Caution sign: Attention in this mode functions like a warning or alert system. It opens up broadly to be receptive to potential risks and threats. This mode is beneficial for scanning the environment for potential dangers, and it has certainly served its purpose in keeping our species alive for thousands of years.

However, if we remain stuck in this mode for too long, it can lead to distractions, anxiety, and hypervigilance. We keep scanning for threat, even when there isn't one. Perhaps we even start to find it. Persistent activation of the caution sign can result in exhaustion, dysfunction, anxiety disorders, and post-traumatic stress disorder (PTSD). This is because this part of our awareness is closely connected to our *physiology* and our fight-or-flight response. When you are stressed, your HPA axis is activated (hypothalamus, pituitary, and adrenal glands), and you set off a cascade of bodily responses. These responses were designed to gear you up for life-saving action—they were not intended to be maintained chronically.

Juggler: This mode of attention is comparable to a juggler managing various tasks. Like a business executive coordinating actions to align with company goals, our attention must competently juggle everything that's important to us. When this mode falters, such as in cases of attention deficit hyperactivity disorder (ADHD), we experience difficulties in maintaining focus and managing multiple tasks effectively. We can also find ourselves overwhelmed or burned out if we feel there are too many tasks to juggle, or else we ... drop a few balls, so to speak.

Paying attention to the way you pay attention is a big part of self-mastery. It makes sense: You can only do better if you are aware of what you are doing in the first place, and the only way to do that is to pay attention not just to the content of your experience, but the way in which you are attending to that content.

How to Improve Your Focus
To improve your focus, the first step is to develop the skill of noticing when your attentional flashlight has wandered away from the task at hand—the task you've

already decided is a choice and priority for you. This exercise involves repeatedly bringing your attention back to the target object whenever it wanders off. Think of it as training a puppy, being consistent and clear with your instructions without being harsh or mean. When you notice your mind wandering, don't indulge in self-criticism or rumination, but simply begin the exercise again. Reframe mind-wandering as a cue to reorient your attention, rather than a failure.

As you practice this exercise, you'll become more attuned to the initial pull of your attention away from the target object, allowing you to bring it back more easily. With improved focus, you'll waste less time, experience fewer mood dips and stress spikes, and worry less when you have important tasks to complete.

Interestingly, as you become better at noticing when your mind has wandered, you'll also learn when it's beneficial to let your mind freely roam, like letting a dog off the leash at a park. This can lead to creative ideas, a sense of good-heartedness, and renewed energy. The important thing is that, in one way or another, you are always aware of what is happening and can switch focus at will.

To find your focus, start with a foundational mindfulness practice called breath awareness. Focus your attention on your breath, and when your mind wanders, gently bring it back. This seemingly simple exercise actually targets all three systems of attention—focusing, noticing, and redirecting—making it an effective cognitive training for attention. By regularly practicing this exercise, you can strengthen your ability to sustain focus and improve your overall attentional skills.

Something else curious happens when you work with this practice. You begin to think of distractions and mind-wanderings in the same way as you do spontaneous emotions or uncomfortable sensations. In just the same way as a flash of anger or a moment of discomfort can cause you to "fuse" with that experience and become trapped there, you can actually learn to recognize a distraction when it appears and choose not to fuse with it, i.e., to keep paying attention to your work.

Again, acceptance and tolerance of your emotions is key here—there is no need for judgment ("your mind has wandered again, you idiot!") because that just prolongs the ninety seconds. Rather, see a distraction for what it is—a distraction. Just because something occurs to you, it doesn't mean you have to follow that thought and get carried away with it. Just because something catches your attention, it doesn't mean it necessarily has to *keep* that attention.

You can begin to see distractions and demands on your attention as buses that are passing you by at a bus stop. Lots of buses will pass you by, each one going in a different direction. But just because a bus passes you, it doesn't mean you have to get on and let it take you with it. If the bus isn't going where you want it to go, just let it pass. Once you get on a bus, be at ease in the traffic where there are lots of different vehicles all going their own way. You don't have to push back against them or judge them. They have their path, you have yours. See them and just come back to what *you* were doing.

Everyday Practice: Finding Your Flashlight

This exercise is not really a question of developing your flashlight—that's because you already have a flashlight, and it's always focused on *something*. Instead, the practice is about gaining awareness over what it's focusing on and then, in time, learning to turn that beam where you want it to shine.

Formal meditation and mindfulness practices are all, in their own slightly different ways, trying to help you master this skill. But here's a secret: You don't need to do formal meditation in this way to learn to take better ownership and mastery of your own conscious attention. In fact, the better you become at this skill, the less necessary it will seem to sit down somewhere and deliberately embark on an activity that is somehow separate from the rest of your experience.

When it comes to working with your flashlight, the key is to practice little windows of awareness, little and often.

Here is a simple exercise you can use in the beginning of your development. But remember that the real goal is not to perform this exercise perfectly; rather, it's to internalize this state of being so that it becomes automatic and spontaneous in the rest of your life.

Get Ready . . .

Sit in an upright, alert posture. Be comfortable but not so relaxed that you are thinking of falling asleep or zoning out. Think "upright," not "uptight." Sit up straight, your shoulders back, chest relaxed and open, in a natural posture that embodies dignity and presence. Try to actually feel what *mastery* and *poise* feels like when expressed in the body.

Let your hands rest neutrally beside you or on the tops of your thighs. Close your eyes or lower them to a soft gaze resting somewhere in the middle distance in front of you. Now breathe. For a moment, follow your breath—this is important: Just follow it. That doesn't mean change it, hold it, or try to force it to conform to your idea of what relaxed and meditative breathing should be. Just imagine for a while that your conscious awareness is tethered to the breath and is watching it peacefully as it comes and goes.

Get Set . . .

To deepen this experience, tune in to any breath-related sensations you become aware of. These may be the coolness of the air going in and out of your nostrils, the sensation of your lungs filling up your chest, your belly moving in and out. Your five senses are your anchors here. Try to adopt an internal posture where there is a sense of nothing to do, nowhere to go, nothing to think about. Just be there with yourself, and all the little flutters your body makes when peacefully at rest.

Next, choose one area of the body—related to whichever breath-related sensations feel most prominent—to focus on for the rest of this exercise. Direct and maintain your attentional focus here, shining that strong beam of the flashlight onto it. Now, this beam is not a harsh interrogation lamp and it's not the limelight on a stage. You are not judging, evaluating, or attaching in any way the sensations you are placing in your awareness. You are just shining the light of awareness on them.

Go!

Now the practice starts in earnest. Almost instantly, you will notice that that flashlight beam starts to weaken and waver and wander somewhere else. This is completely normal. It's not a mistake, but something your brain will just do. Your job is to notice it and gently tilt that flashlight back to where you placed it originally. That's all.

The real magic of this exercise is not in how perfectly focused you can keep your attention. Rather, it's about how you are able to pull it back again when it invariably does. Think of it like this: You build muscle in the gym when you constantly fight against gravity—the goal is never to lift the weight once and hold it up with ease. "Training" your attention happens in the same way—every time you bring your attention back, you haven't failed, but rather completed one "rep" and taught yourself that skill so that next time it's easier and more automatic.

You may learn to identify a whole array of distractions that can pull your attention away:

- Memories from the past and the string of thoughts that triggers, all falling like dominoes one after the other
- Spontaneous physical sensations—a grumbly stomach or an itch
- Outside noises, smells, etc.
- Worries and ruminations, perhaps about what you have to do next, what's happening tomorrow . . .
- Judgments—for example, "this is boring" or "you suck at this exercise"
- Analyzing and evaluating—for example, starting to think about the theory behind this exercise, intellectualizing, getting bogged down in detail thinking *about* the exercise rather than *doing* the exercise . . .

The truth is, your brain can seemingly invent four thousand different distractions every minute to pull that attention away. For your purposes, none of this matters. It's of no consequence. You don't have to follow those thoughts and decide what you think of them (because that's just another distraction!), and you don't need to get carried away chastising yourself every time you lose attention (because, again, that's just another way to lose attention).

Just think of returning the flashlight to where you placed it with a gentle nudge. Even if you notice your attention has been wandering for a long time, it doesn't matter. **What matters is returning.** For some people, a word or sound is easier to focus on than a body part. Just experiment with what works for you, but don't jump around from technique to technique. It *won't* be easy at first, whatever your point of focus, but that's the point. The task will not get easier, but you will get better at it.

The Arrow Model of Focus

Of course, awareness and focused attention are not a flashlight—that's just a useful metaphor. Another metaphor that you may find useful is to think of focus as an arrow. This metaphor can help us gain an understanding of the neurochemical aspects of motivation, attention, and focus.

This metaphorical arrow is made of two parts: the shaft and the arrowhead.

The shaft of the arrow represents *epinephrine* (adrenaline), which increases energy and alertness . . . but does not directly increase focus. Epinephrine is necessary for focus, but on its own it's not sufficient.

The arrowhead represents *acetylcholine*, which activates specific neurons and directs the focus to a particular location—a sharp, single point. Acetylcholine is responsible for concentration and focus.

Now, to *sustain* focus, dopamine is required, and we can loosely think of dopamine as a "molecule of motivation." You can imagine that in our metaphor, dopamine is everything that is binding the arrowhead to the shaft and keeping it together.

Though this is admittedly a very simplified model of the physiology behind what we explored in our flashlight practice, it's nevertheless a helpful way to visualize what is going on for us when we say "I can't focus" or "I'm not feeling motivated."

The combination of acetylcholine, epinephrine, and dopamine allows for precise and prolonged focus. With all three, we have enough energy, focus, and sustained motivation to set goals and reach them, or to muster our mental resources long enough to properly process and master our world.

Without epinephrine, we are lethargic—like an arrow that has no shaft, we lack any force or thrust behind our goals, no matter how well defined they are.

Without acetylcholine we are scattered and useless—like an arrow that has no point. We can fling ourselves with energy and motivation into new tasks, but we lack effectiveness because that energy just dissipates if it can't be focused onto one specific point.

Without dopamine we lack discipline and consistency—we are like the perfect arrow that nonetheless crumbles to nothing within a few minutes. We may have the initial spark to do something, and know what we have to do . . . we just can't sustain motivation long enough to do it.

So, what's the point of this elaborate metaphor? Well, if we understand exactly where our own arrow is failing and why, we can take reasonable steps to fix the problem (which, let's be honest, may be a combination of all three!). There are three broad approaches we can take to improve each of these aspects of attention. Let's take a look:

Strategy 1: Increase Epinephrine Levels

Epinephrine plays a crucial role in providing energy and alertness. If you are lacking drive, energy, and impetus, you may need to take action to increase your epinephrine levels. To encourage your brain to release this essential neurotransmitter, you can engage in activities that naturally boost adrenaline . . . such as drinking coffee!

A few things to bear in mind, though: Caffeine can create a feeling of wakefulness and alertness because it activates the adenosine and epinephrine systems. This can improve mental and physical focus, provided you take a good dose—somewhere between two hundred to four hundred milligrams, which is around two cups of normal coffee, but can vary considerably according to how its brewed.

Find your own preferred level (everyone's caffeine tolerance is different) but try to avoid having coffee within the first ninety to one hundred twenty minutes of waking. This is the period of time when your body naturally produces wakefulness hormones to rouse you from sleep, and adding caffeine on top of this can be overstimulating and counterproductive. Caffeine also enhances the density and efficacy of the dopamine receptors in the brain, so it serves more than one function.

Finally, as you're probably already aware, avoid taking coffee after about 4 p.m., since it delays and disrupts the quality of your sleep. Misuse of caffeine may actually harm your neurochemistry over time, so be moderate. You should only seldom have three or more cups in one day, and save them for the morning hours.

Dr. Andrew Huberman is a professor of neurobiology and ophthalmology at Stanford University School of Medicine, and his work focuses on neural health and optimal brain performance. He believes that "stress itself can increase the ability to focus and concentrate"—and it does this by stimulating epinephrine release. Whenever you feel really fired up and energized to do a task, it's because epinephrine is there, giving you a boost. Though most of us tend to think of stress as a bad thing, acute stress is actually good for the immune system and helps us fixate on things, making us better problem-solvers and more creative, inspired thinkers.

You can leverage this "healthy stress" by consciously creating a sense of challenge for yourself—which can be reframed as a mild sense of discomfort. Make things a game; dare yourself to go a little further or do a little more. Set up deadlines for yourself. Don't go too easy on yourself. One method is to try a cold shower for one to five minutes to give you both an epinephrine and a dopamine boost. It's guaranteed you'll feel alert and refreshed afterward!

Of course, you don't want to cultivate stress to the extent that you chronically strain yourself, creating overwhelm, burnout, or apathy. Just find that slight edge that fires *you* up. You don't want to allow yourself to get too comfortable (the Spartans, who we will discuss shortly, knew all this well before the advent of neuroscience!). Exactly what you do to maintain this alertness/discomfort is up to you, but remember: relaxation and ease will *not* increase epinephrine levels! That means if you are lacking energy and are feeling uninspired, you will probably not help yourself with conventional "self-care" or taking a break.

Strategy 2: Increase Acetylcholine Levels

As we've said, energy is necessary for focused attention . . . but it's not sufficient. To introduce yet another metaphor, energy is like fuel in the tank of a car. We definitely need it for the journey we're going on, but the journey can't be made unless there's a clear plan of where we're actually headed—for that we need a driver who has a map and can keep the car on the road long enough to get us there.

Acetylcholine is the neurochemical that helps harness the drive and energy you have and train it toward one point, directing your focus to specific areas or tasks. Acetylcholine manages and moderates sensory input, helping you decide what's important in your experience and what to tune out. In fact, when you practice the flashlight exercise in the previous section, this is precisely the capability you are learning to work with— sharpening your arrowpoint, as it were.

There are many ways to increase acetylcholine levels in the brain.

- **Visualization exercises:** For thirty seconds to a few minutes, pick an object in your line of sight and just train your brain to focus on it, to the exclusion of everything else in your environment. You may recognize that this is just an eyes-open, visual variant of the flashlight exercise. Do this exercise several times throughout the day and notice how quickly your attention improves in all other areas.

- **Create a distraction-free environment:** Whatever your task is, try to deliberately set up a working environment that gives your attention the best chance. If you physically and literally clear your space of clutter and distractions, it's easier to mentally do the same. Clear your desk, get rid of phones, and install apps to block you from browsing mindlessly online. Close the door, stick up a "do not disturb" sign, and let everyone know to leave you in peace for a certain period.

- **Diets and supplements:** You can actually increase acetylcholine levels directly by eating things like egg yolks. More broadly, a healthy diet will sustain your body's natural balance. It's not that a good diet will magically make you pay attention, but rather that no amount of willpower or mindfulness practice will cancel out a poor diet.

Before we continue, a word on nicotine: Smoking is actually one way to boost acetylcholine levels, and probably explains why people become addicted—it helps them stay alert and focused and quickly becomes a crutch to aid in emotional self-regulation. Of course, smoking comes with so many downsides nobody would recommend nicotine as a performance-enhancing drug! But what we do know is that if you are a smoker, your brain may have come to depend on the nicotine. That means that when you're quitting, you need to pay extra attention to how you're going to modulate your acetylcholine levels without it. People might not think that meditation makes a good cigarette substitute, but the research does suggest that it can be!

Strategy 3: Regulate Dopamine Levels

Dopamine is a complicated and much misunderstood neurotransmitter, but it's broadly associated with the pleasure, reward, and motivation circuits in the brain and is thus an important component of how we sustain ongoing focus and motivation.

There is much advice out there on how to do a "dopamine detox" and so on, but it's not simply a question of achieving the right level in the body that would lead to optimal motivation. It's a little like saying that we ought to find the best level of progesterone for a woman's body—it doesn't make any sense because when a woman's hormonal cycles are balanced and healthy, they *change* throughout the month. What matters is how that progesterone is *functioning* holistically. It's the same with dopamine; you seldom need to boost flagging levels or detox from too-high levels. Instead, **it's about supporting the entire organism to better modulate its own functional levels within certain parameters—which is something your body knows how to do if it's healthy.**

Therefore, if you want to optimize dopamine levels, the solution tends to be simply to ensure you're as healthy as you can be. You can certainly eat foods rich in tyrosine (meat, Parmesan cheese, certain vegetables, seeds, and nuts), drink caffeine, meditate, and take cold showers. But other conventional health advice will probably bring you the greatest gains:

- Exercise regularly.
- Eat enough protein. (Most Americans actually eat too much protein; few in the modern world are deficient in this macronutrient.)

- Reduce consumption of saturated fat (like animal fat, butter, palm oil, coconut oil) since it can disrupt dopamine signaling.
- Maintain good gut health since your gut is a prime site for neurotransmitter creation. (Incidentally, the nutrient most Americans *are* deficient in is gut-healthy fiber.)
- Get enough high-quality sleep. It's not enough to just count the hours—sleep varies enormously in quality. Lack of good sleep can interfere with proper dopamine release the next morning.
- Get enough sun exposure and spend time in nature.
- Make sure you don't have any vitamin or mineral supplements, which could interfere with your body's ability to synthesize dopamine. Iron and vitamin B6 are important.

One thing we can take away from the arrow model of attention is to remind ourselves that **the "mind" is, ultimately, the function of our physical body.** Thoughts are behaviors that are occurring in the flesh and blood tissues of our brains. Ideas and feelings are measurable changes in the cells of our organs—and the brain is not the only organ implicated.

It can be tempting to forget this when we talk about abstract things like "attention" and "drive" and "motivation." But all of these are inextricably linked to our embodied selves. There is no such thing as willpower if the body has no glucose from which to make it! Similarly, our feelings of self-mastery mean nothing if our body does not have the micronutrients from which to synthesize the neurotransmitter that our experience of self-mastery is dependent on. Long story short: your body is the foundation for your entire experience. If you want better self-discipline, attention, and so on, maintaining the health of your body is non-negotiable.

Spartan Discipline—Improvement by Subtraction

Let's return once again to our flashlight of attention. When it's shining on one particular thing, something else is happening— everything outside of that beam is in darkness. It might as well not exist, right? You can say that the thing inside your beam is your priority, and everything else is of no consequence.

Think of someone you consider a leader in their field. Consider any world-famous authors, celebrities, politicians, and so on. You can likely identify them by that *one thing* that makes them stand out from the crowd. What you might not notice, however, is that their ability to distinguish themselves in this way comes in no small part from the fact that they have not spent any time on any other skill or trait.

Pick a notable entrepreneur and discover that their private lives are poorly developed; notice that the famous physicist is in poor physical shape and never learned to swim; realize, maybe, that the paradigm-shifting artist and activist is a sensation all over the media, but has nothing in their bank account.

You get the idea: Success comes down to a kind of self-discipline, and that self-discipline is not just about taking action but also about not taking other actions. The flashlight shines brightly because its light is not spread diffusely, but targeted. The famous people you imagined have an even narrower and tighter focus: Theirs is the proverbial laser, and it excludes even more in its supreme focus on *just one* goal.

The Spartans were famous for their unique philosophies, one of which was a

pronounced dedication to doing less of what is harmful or unproductive, rather than solely focusing on doing more good. It's a perspective shift that radically changes things. You can be a generalist and achieve average success in a million different areas. Or, you could be a specialist and pour all your resources into just one goal—where it has the chance of going further.

The mindset requires you **to think carefully about what you won't do**. It also shifts your thinking to carefully eliminating everything that you already know is a waste of time or else unlikely to have a large enough impact to warrant your attention. For instance, Warren Buffett's investment strategy emphasizes avoiding bad investments rather than predicting future successes. Elon Musk similarly told people that "you should take the approach that you're wrong. Your goal is to be less wrong." Therefore, we are growing by elimination; finding the good by steadily and gradually removing the bad.

In your own life, you can apply this principle by understanding that self-discipline is more about what you choose not to do. Instead of seeking a miraculous workout or following the latest diet trend, focus on consistently going to the gym and avoiding unhealthy foods. **The idea is to prioritize avoiding small losses rather than chasing big gains.**

This Spartan approach to discipline, **known as improvement by subtraction,** is exemplified by an anecdote from ancient Sparta. When questioned about why they entrusted their fields to non-citizen peasants, a Spartan king responded that they achieved their success not by tending to the fields but by focusing on themselves. This quote highlights the Spartan culture of self-cultivation and their commitment to focus. It reminds us that we don't need to do everything ourselves and that it is essential to prioritize our time and efforts wisely.

The Spartans understood the value of specialization and honing their skills. They didn't waste time on trivial tasks or penny-pinching activities that didn't align with their goals. Instead, they dedicated themselves to perfecting their chosen craft. This disciplined and focused approach led to their reputation as one of history's most efficient and formidable military forces. The ancient world acknowledged the exceptional skill and worth of a single Spartan compared to several soldiers from other states.

According to James Clear, the distinction we are making here is between **improvement by addition versus improvement by subtraction**. Improvement by addition is focused on doing more of what does work: producing a faster car, creating a more powerful speaker, building a stronger table. Improvement by subtraction is focused on doing less of what doesn't work: eliminating mistakes, reducing complexity, and stripping away the inessential.

How could you apply these concepts to your own life when it comes to self-discipline?

Meet Chris, who is trying to become more disciplined in his life. He wakes up and gets to work cleaning up the house from the day before. He hates this chore, but to make it easier, he puts on headphones so he can listen to a self-improvement podcast. He gives himself a little reward at the end to keep up his motivation. Later, he spends time hunting around for clean, presentable clothes (he has to quickly iron a shirt) and dawdles a bit trying to decide which shoes to pair with it so that he gives the right impression in the meeting he's heading to.

After work he heads to a new yoga class that he's trying. He's not sure it's actually having any benefit, but he's already paid so he's giving it a chance. When he gets home, he wastes a few hours on YouTube, then makes dinner (oops—he forgets an ingredient and has to step out to the store for a moment to get it) and then spends forty-five minutes cooking a healthy meal. He watches two hours of TV, eats a candy bar he later regrets, then goes to bed.

Chris has dreams—he wants to make his amazing idea for a children's book a reality, he wants to meet someone special, and he wants to lose a few pounds and get into shape. Yet every evening he gets the sinking sensation that these things might never happen. How is it that he feels like he works hard all day, only to never really advance?

Now meet Christina. You could say Christina is *obsessed* with her current project. She's retraining in a completely new career and has grand ideas for a life she wants to build for herself. She wakes up early in the morning, and the first thing she does is hit the books for her course. She had already told herself that for the four months it takes to complete this course, she won't even acknowledge that housework exists. She pays a cleaner once a week and lives with the mess the rest of the time.

At work she is strategic—she has identified only those things that are compatible with the overarching goal. Everything else she lets go without guilt or even a second thought. For exercise she runs after work—not because she's mad about running, but because it keeps her healthy and de-stressed enough to focus on her main obsession. She may find another style of exercise she likes more later, maybe. What she definitely won't do is waste time on something she already knows she hates—like yoga. Running is good enough for now, so she does it with the same discipline as she brushes her teeth every morning.

She wears basically the same thing every morning, eats simple and nutritious batch-cooked meals (basically beans, rice, eggs, and a few veggies), and simply refuses to waste a second on things like TV or mindless scrolling online. This doesn't really require any willpower, as such—there's nothing in Christina's home to tempt or distract her, so nothing she needs willpower to pull her away from. Basically, she has no choice. There are no unhealthy snacks in the kitchen, and there's no material in her study except that which is required to complete her course. She has essentially disabled her internet at home, and her phone is always on silent and in another room. All her groceries are delivered to her house on a pre-ordered schedule, so she doesn't have to think about that.

Within four months, Christina is exhausted—but she has completed her course and has a whole new career set off on the right foot. And she did it with the same level of energy that Chris has—only she focused it on ONE goal. As Bruce Lee said, "The successful warrior is the average man with laser-like focus."

Author Victor Hugo told his servant to hide his clothes for a specific period every day to force him to just sit down and write. He completed the *Hunchback of Notre Dame* naked—he had no choice! Only once he had completed his assigned writing for the day was he allowed to have clothes again to go about his day.

Herman Melville actually asked his wife to chain him to his desk so that he would have no choice but to finish his novel *Moby Dick*. Psychiatrist Carl Jung spent long days isolated in a small stone tower in the woods. It had no electricity, no running water, and not even carpets or floorboards. Sure, Jung could have tried all sorts of self-discipline gimmicks to stop himself from wasting time—or he could just swiftly remove the option so that he had no choice but to focus.

The Spartans had a goal so singular that the entire nation shared it: supreme military mastery. They succeeded. In fact, they succeeded so well that their memory still lingers in the minds and hearts of people today.

Simplicity breeds success. Keep that arrowhead focused and get rid of everything else. It's not important. The more you can hack away at the inessential, the more room and energy you will have for massive achievement on those tasks you have identified as worth it. Don't let trivial things trip you up—you cannot optimize on the unimportant. If something doesn't ultimately matter, don't waste time trying to coax yourself to do it better. Simply don't do it!

Henry David Thoreau said, "Our life is frittered away by detail. Simplify, simplify." He was right. The corollary is that if we wish not to waste our lives, we need to get really good at identifying and dismissing the irrelevant details of life. Be bold and disciplined in what you refuse to grant your attention and energy. You are just one person, with finite resources—where do you want to spend them? **Make a "budget" for your life force and follow through.**

You can only live *one* life. Even though certain paths might be interesting or valuable, are they the most valuable for **you**? If you could choose only one, what would it be? Now, have the discipline to withdraw all energy wasted on tasks that are not related, and reinvest them where they can make a big difference. You will never again say that you don't have the time. **If you are focused, there is enough time.**

Summary:

- It's possible to harness your mind power and use it to work for you, rather than constantly living at its mercy, or even having it work against you.
- People tend to procrastinate because they don't feel like they are in the right mood to complete the task, and they believe that their mood will change in the near future. But this sets up a procrastination "doom loop" that continuously reinforces itself. Perfectionism, fear of success/failure, and

a powerless mindset all exacerbate the problem.

- To get out of the loop requires plenty of self-compassion, learning how to reframe our thinking around the task (focus on values, not shortcomings), and taking small, meaningful steps toward our goal. It's about mood and energy management, not time management or organization.

- Your attention operates in three modes: flashlight (orienting system), caution sign (alerting system), and juggler (executive functioning). To master self-discipline, develop the mindfulness skill of noticing when your attentional flashlight has wandered away from the task at hand, and bring it gently back without judgment.

- The arrow model of focus explains the role of epinephrine, acetylcholine, and dopamine in driving, focusing, and sustaining our attentional awareness, respectively. To improve self-discipline, increase/modulate these levels using meditation and visualization techniques, "good stress," caffeine, and healthy lifestyle choices.

- Finally, the Spartans can teach us about discipline by subtraction rather than addition, i.e., what we choose not to focus on. Think carefully about what is irrelevant or harmful, and void those tasks. You have finite resources, so be strategic with them and simplify—if you do so, there will be enough time and energy to achieve your dreams.

Chapter Four: Self-Discipline, Today and Forever

You already have everyday habits that you follow without thinking about it—the question is whether you choose to make those habits ones that align with your goals.

You already have a mindset that colors everything in your world—the question is how you choose to shape that mindset and use it as a tool.

You already have attention—the question is whether you can consciously choose where that attention lands, and how long to keep it there.

By this same principle, your body has certain limits, preferences, and patterns built in—the question is whether you can work **with** these patterns or work **against** them.

In this final chapter, we're looking at what self-discipline looks like in the long term. Many people can find it easy to muster up dedication . . . as long as they don't have to maintain it for longer than a month or so! They may hear the word "discipline" and imagine it's a bit like the mindset of going on a diet, i.e., something painful and unsustainable that you only keep up for as long as you need to and then drop as soon as you can.

But those among us who are truly disciplined know that it's a long life, and staying consistently disciplined *forever* requires a little more than doing dramatic overnight transformations that only leave you back at square one in a few weeks or months. Specifically, it requires a clear-headed acknowledgement of the fact that you will mess up, and strategies to work with that fact.

It's all about expectation. If you have a vision of a disciplined life that looks like perfection, ease, all-or-nothing thinking, and constant improvement day after day, you're going to give up at the first hurdle! Rather, disciplined and effective people have figured out how to work with their "failures," their lack of motivation, their bad days, and their unexpected setbacks. They are never surprised when things don't go to plan—in fact, they expect it and have already set up a plan to not only persist but to turn that adversity to their advantage.

We'll be looking at ways to work around your natural physical limitations to get the most out of your energy and attention levels, as well as how to structure your day-to-day life so that no obstacles, snags, or disappointments ever have the power to derail you completely. It's not about invulnerability or perfection, but rather about flexibility, learning, and a slow-but-steady approach that breeds success in the real world.

Working with Your Ultradian Rhythms

Sometimes, the most disciplined thing you can do is take a nap.

If that seems surprising to you, consider that just because action is valuable, it doesn't mean that it's always the best thing to do at every moment. Rest is valuable, too, and in a way it's the other side of the productivity coin—when we rest, we consolidate, refresh ourselves, and pause to digest what we've learned. By sometimes doing nothing, we are more effective when we are active.

This is why it's worth abandoning the all-or-nothing, "no pain no gain" style of thinking that tells you that the only way to achieve is to *go go go*, and that the only valid way to respond to fatigue is to blast through it with sheer force of will.

Our bodies, in their wisdom, will tell us clearly when we need a break. If we listen, we can learn to interpret these signals (drowsiness, loss of focus, hunger, fidgetiness) for what they are, rather than assuming that we lack discipline and then ignoring them. We've already mentioned the ultra-high achievers in the world and the value of their relentless drive and singular focus. A common but less discussed part of this story is also burnout, exhaustion, and even illness.

So let's explore this, then, with a firm understanding of why we're doing it: not to be kind to ourselves in some vague way (although we should be!) but rather because **moderation is actually smarter, more effective, and more elegant than the alternative.**

For a crude example, it would be pretty stupid to force yourself to wake up at 2:30 a.m. and do a big sweaty workout and some complicated calculus problems before going back to bed. It's a bad idea for two reasons: First you will perform so poorly it's hardly worth your while, and second it'll be really, really unpleasant!

So, discipline is not just managing your mindset, habits, and attention. It's also about managing the **timing** and coordination of your life.

Circadian rhythms are the body's twenty-four-hour cycles that respond to changes in the environment. They regulate various processes and behaviors in humans, such as energy levels, digestion, hormone release, sleep patterns, and mood. Researchers have studied circadian rhythms in different organisms and found that environmental factors like light, temperature, food, exercise, and social connections can affect genes responsible for regulating these rhythms.

Depending on your mindset, this is either a problem or an opportunity. If you can learn to listen to your body and work with it, you will increase your sense of productivity and well-being. If not, you're making your own

biological realties something to fight against—
and that's pretty tiring.

Cycling within the circadian rhythms are
smaller cycles—ultradian rhythms. These
occur many times in a day and are shorter in
duration, approximately on a roughly ninety-
minute cycle. Sleep researcher Nathaniel
Kleitman discovered in the 1950s that the
body tends to move through ninety-to-one-
hundred-twenty-minute cycles, and framed
these cycles as oscillations between activity
and rest states.

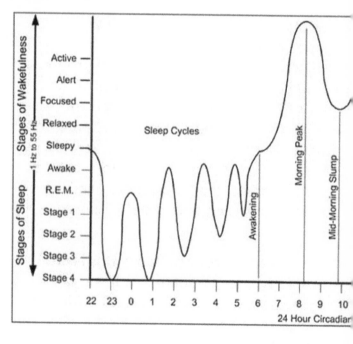

So, there is a morning peak at around 8 a.m., followed by a second peak just before noon, one at around 2:30 and again at 5:30. These peaks tend to be less and less intense as the day wears on, finishing with a peak just before 8 p.m. Each of these peaks is followed by a slump roughly ninety to one hundred twenty minutes later, and so the cycle repeats. Overnight, the same patterns follow but more subdued, and can be seen in the various sleep stages.

Energy Management, Not Time Management

The fact is that biologically, we are programmed to be most efficient, alert, creative, sociable, and active during the peaks, and less so during the slumps that follow. It doesn't take a genius to see that if you, for example, scheduled all your difficult work to be completed during slumps, and your rest periods during your energy peaks, you'd be badly out of whack and likely wouldn't achieve much.

Do the opposite, however, and you are operating at the very upper limits of what is possible for you, biologically speaking. The great thing about this extra boost is that you don't actually have to work any harder to unlock it—you just have to carefully plan when you'll do the same amount of work. If productivity and efficiency are important to you, then mastering your ultradian rhythms is definitely one of the lowest hanging fruits!

This requires a mindset shift: **There is no virtue or value in pushing yourself against your body's natural rhythms.** You are not going to develop rock-hard discipline or train yourself to be better—you're just going to wear yourself out.

Your entire organism has evolved to work in ninety-to-one-hundred-twenty-minute sprints followed by a rest period. That means if you push your work window to four hours instead of around two, not only are those latter two hours going to be spent grinding through when your body would rather rest, but you will also be more fatigued by the time your *next* peak arrives, and so unable to take proper advantage of it. It's like trying to lift a heavy bar while you are standing on the other end of it! You are spending plenty of effort—but how much of that effort is just working against yourself?

Now, you're probably wondering if the cycle is the same for everyone. The answer is that it's broadly the same, although you may have *slight* differences. The best way to find out is to observe yourself for a week at least and notice when you feel most alert (not just mentally, but in every way). The start of each cycle is triggered by fluctuations in the glucocorticoid system, which regulates cortisol release (this is why it's important not to drink coffee immediately upon waking—you're taking a hit of energy on what is likely already the highest energy peak of the day, and it can be damaging to your hormones). Be careful, though—if you have a habit of ignoring your own cycles, you may have a mistaken idea of what's natural for you. Many people who claim that they're not "morning people" are actually just chronically exhausted or have poor sleep habits that have become ingrained over the years.

Once you've noticed when your first peak naturally starts to happen, try to reserve this moment for your most challenging and intensive work. Have your priority clearly identified and schedule the hardest tasks first (more on this in a later chapter). Similarly, you can schedule other tasks accordingly. For example, less demanding admin tasks can be done near the end of the day. You don't *need* to be ultra focused here, so don't waste your peak period on things that don't require your mental best.

Most people will manage around four ninety-minute blocks of focused, deep work a day, at the very upper limit. This may surprise you, since it seems very little. But **if you do deep, quality, and focused work, it tends not to take as much time**. Likewise, if you take a closer look at the claim that people can work for a solid eight hours a day, you'll likely find that very little of this is focused, deep work.

Let's take a closer look at what happens within this ninety-to-one-hundred-twenty-minute period. The structure can be broken down like this:

- The first part: arousal
- The second part: peak performance
- The final part: stress

So, within these cycles, you have *another* cycle. It may take around five to fifteen minutes to warm up, then about an hour of good, solid, deep work that really moves you forward toward your goals. Your focus may waver a bit here and there, but you are most able at this point to pull it back again. The final part of the period you are winding down and beginning to notice signs that it's time to rest.

Your attention, focus, and discipline are just as much about what you do **during** your peak period as what you do **after** it. Try to think of resting after work as *a part of* that work. It's during this period that you rest and consolidate. Sleep at night is when your brain literally reconfigures itself—i.e., you learn.

If you can, take a twenty-minute break, but even a small break is better than nothing. Try doing something radically different—for example, if you've been thinking hard, get outside and have a brisk walk in the sunshine and fresh air. Leave the room, change posture, and try to literally imagine your brain changing gears.

Leveraging Your Ultradian Cycles

- **Rework your schedule:** It's not always possible to change things to exactly what would suit us, but do your best to make your schedule fit your cycles, not the other way around.

- **Take breaks:** After each ninety-minute cycle of focused work, take a break to recharge. It's important not to exceed two to four cycles per day to prevent exhaustion. Use these breaks for deliberate decompression, allowing your mind to relax and recharge before the next cycle.

- **Embrace occasional distractions and regain focus:** Accept that distractions will occasionally occur, and what matters is your ability to refocus. When distractions arise, make a conscious effort to bring your attention back to the task at hand. Developing the skill to quickly regain focus is key to maintaining productivity throughout the day.

- **Make your breaks REAL breaks:** Don't worry about what's happening when the break is over. Don't try to cram something in so you can have a break while still being productive. It's better to have a ten-minute *real* break than a twenty-minute break where you're only pretending to rest!

- **Have boundaries, and respect them yourself:** Know when to stop. Work can be infinite if you let it be, but your resources are not infinite. Learn to say no. Let go of the idea that you haven't done "enough." Aim for eight percent of perfection and let the rest go, or you risk falling into the diminishing returns trap (i.e., more and more effort just brings smaller and smaller gains).

- **Use nature to help you:** Immediately upon waking, take a deep breath of fresh air by an open window, and shine sunshine into your eyes (if you can). This helps modulate your sleep/wake cycles and can be profoundly energizing.

- **Plan hard exercise for your peak periods:** And plan more moderate exercise for smaller peaks.

Remember, the number of focused bouts you can perform in a day will depend on various factors, such as the quality of your sleep and how easily you enter a focused state. Your cycles will run regardless, so you might as well learn to work with them. Also remember that the cycle goes daily, whether it's the weekend or not! That means it's probably not worth your while to have a "rest day" on the weekend that actually just throws your cycles out of whack.

Your Pre-game Routine

Understanding ultradian rhythms means we understand that there will be energy peaks and energy troughs every day, and choosing to work with that. More broadly, self-disciplined people understand something else, namely that **there will be times of motivation, and there will be times when you can barely muster any ineptest or motivation for even your most cherished goals.**

Now, in the same way that being tired doesn't mean you lack discipline (it just means you need to rest), occasionally feeling unmotivated doesn't mean that you lack discipline either. It simply means that motivation levels rise and fall, and it's perfectly normal. We can always take breaks, reassess, adjust, and so on . . . without it meaning that something is wrong or that we should abandon our goal entirely.

A good example concerns weight loss. Someone may have a clear goal and excellent habits that are going to bring them to that goal, but one day, they reach a weight loss plateau and appear not to lose any more weight. They lose motivation and feel like they want to give up entirely since their ordinary methods are "not working."

But *they* are working. This person has just failed to realize that this is what the weight loss path tends to look like: fits and starts, with plenty of plateaus followed by sudden improvements. Whether you stay the course or abandon it comes down to your attitude to the guaranteed *fact* of future adversity, difficulty, and challenge along the way. Are you expecting that it will be difficult at some points, or are you sincerely planning to maintain strong, stable motivation throughout?

That's a rather long way of saying something simple: **Developing self-discipline doesn't mean the path magically gets easier**. It doesn't mean you suddenly don't have days where you wake up completely unmotivated to do anything. What it does mean is that you are prepared for them and refuse to let them be a reason for you to give up. You will instantly grow more resilient and adaptable the moment you acknowledge that yes, parts of your journey to your goal are going to be unpleasant, confusing, and demoralizing. This way, when that situation arises, you're not caught off guard. You don't give up. In fact, you see the adversity as positive proof that you are doing something special: pushing against your limits, growing, developing. That's a good thing!

What to Do When You Just Aren't Motivated

You can hack your biorhythms all you like, take supplements, live an ultra-clean and wholesome lifestyle, have pristine mental health, and meditate twenty-four hours a day. . . and still find yourself struggling to muster motivation some days. That's because change is, and always will be, hard. If it wasn't, you would have done it by now, right? And so would everyone else. Self-discipline doesn't spare you from the occasional moments of grinding through—it just better equips you to push right through them.

One thing that sets baseball apart from most other sports is the significant number of games played. Major League Baseball teams have a 162-game season, which is twice as many as the NBA and ten times more than the NFL. Even high school baseball players typically have forty to sixty games each year.

With such a large number of games, there will inevitably be days when motivation is lacking, the body feels tired, or one is simply not mentally prepared for the game. In this way, baseball reflects aspects of life, where there are days when important things feel like a struggle.

However, regardless of one's feelings, the game must be played. Finding a solution to overcome the lack of motivation becomes crucial. Many athletes use a "pre-game routine" as a way to pull themselves out of a funk and reach a state where they can perform well no matter what.

The pre-game routine involves specific actions like jogging, stretching, tossing the ball, and pitching practice. This routine not only warms up the body but, more importantly, prepares the mind for competition. By consistently following this routine, even if lacking initial motivation, the player enters the desired "game mode."

The concept of a routine is not limited to baseball but can be applied to other areas of life. Successful individuals in various fields have their own rituals before important tasks, such as NBA players before free throws, comedians before going on stage, or corporate executives with morning meditation. These routines help them get into the right mental state even when motivation is low.

By adopting a similar process, anyone can overcome the motivation threshold and consistently perform essential tasks, whether it's exercising, studying, writing, speaking, or any other important endeavor. And the great thing is that the routine can be done whether you feel like it or not!

Developing your own version of this routine is easy.

Step 1: Make it easy

You want to make starting your routine so automatic and obvious that there really is no real way to say no to it. It should be something you can slip into almost without thinking about it.

Some examples:

- Your study routine starts by getting a glass of water. It's the easiest thing in the world to get a glass of water, right?
- Your gym routine starts by just putting on your gym shoes. Easy. It's even easier when those shoes are in arm's reach and there aren't any other shoes to put on, even if you wanted to.
- Your piano practice routine starts just after you fetch a coffee and walk past the piano. You can't help it—you have

to walk past the piano to get anywhere in the house!

Often, a lack of motivation is nothing more than a little inertia stopping you from *starting*. Once you start, you may find you just carry on fairly easily. The hardest part is just to get going, but luckily you can get going with really small actions. What you don't want to do is build up your routine as some dreadful, monumental thing. Rather, ease into it. Some people get their run done in the early hours. They wake up to go to the bathroom, and on their way back, they immediately step into their running shoes that are right next to the front door, and once that's done it's just a few more automatic steps to go out the door and begin their run. This happens so quickly they are basically already running before they've had a chance to wake up and start convincing themselves of all the reasons they can't.

True, you'll need a little push even for small tasks at first, but tell yourself, "I'm just putting on my shoes. That's all." Don't even think about the next step. "I'm just doing five minutes. That's all I have to do."

Step 2: Get moving . . . literally

You cannot think yourself into motivation. You need to literally *move your body*—even if your goals and tasks are purely intellectual. To understand why this is, just consider what your body does when you are feeling unmotivated. Not much!

Lacking mental and emotional energy manifests in lacking physical energy, so you slouch and slump. You don't move. But the opposite is also true—if you move, you can influence your thoughts and feelings toward movement, too. It's so much easier to feel that you're *moving* toward your goal when your body is literally moving.

That's why so many people find that a long walk alone helps them solve problems—the motion of their feet moves them forward so they can start finding a more abstract way to move forward. Your motivation and energy can follow your physical actions. We tend to think that if we are happy, for example, we smile—but it goes the other way around, too. If you smile, you feel happy. So smile!

Let's say you're trying to motivate yourself to write a difficult essay. Your pre-game routine should be easy to start, and involve you moving somehow. Activity doesn't just mean exercise, though. In this case, it can simply mean that you are doing something that brings you closer to *physically* writing that essay. This could be sitting down with pen and paper and brainstorming something. Just *thinking* about what you will do . . . not so much.

Step 3: Be consistent

Follow the exact same formula each and every time. You're building a habit, because if something is a habit, it gets done automatically and without any extra effort—precisely what you want when you're low on motivation! When you automate your actions through habit, you save time and energy—which you can better invest in those tasks that bring you to your goal.

What you want to do with your pre-game routine is teach your brain to expect certain outcomes and anticipate them as givens. "This is how I do XYZ, this comes first, and then the next thing is this . . ." The actions you take become a matter of course rather than something you need to consciously choose again and again. Every day you probably wake up and brush your teeth or put on clothes. You never need to really force yourself or dig around for motivation to do these things. You do them just because . . . well, that's what you do. You've always done that.

It's *that* level of automaticity that you are trying to build with your pre-game routine. That feeling that doing your tasks is just inevitable. You want to set up a life so that not doing your pre-game routine feels more difficult than just doing it.

Do the Big Thing First

There are many variations of the technique we're about to discuss, but to summarize them all simply, it's this: **Do the big thing first.**

The "eat the frog" technique is a well-known time-management strategy that taps into our internal clocks (the ultradian rhythms we already explored) to boost productivity. It suggests tackling the most challenging or important task first thing in the morning when we typically have higher energy and motivation, but it's also a *psychological* trick, because it empowers us to tackle tasks that might otherwise hang over us and create dread and resistance . . . and procrastination.

The "eat the frog" concept suggests tackling unpleasant but important tasks on your to-do list. The idea is that if you absolutely *had* to eat a frog, your best strategy is probably to eat it as quickly as possible and get it over and done with! A corollary is that, if you did eat that frog, everything else in that day would feel like a breeze ...

These tasks, referred to as "frog" tasks, often require effort and are easy to put off. However, these big gnarly tasks also bring corresponding benefits once accomplished. For example, engaging in a challenging morning run may be initially difficult to start, but the post-run "runner's high" can enhance the rest of the day . . . not to mention make tomorrow's run that little bit easier.

The term "frog" doesn't assign negativity to the task itself, but rather highlights the importance of addressing tasks that require effort to avoid potential long-term consequences. With a procrastinator's mindset, these are precisely the tasks that would trigger a sense of avoidance, but this technique asks you to continually turn that on its head and start to **consider these tasks as the most important and valuable priorities of the day.**

Eat the Frog!
Step 1: Find your "frog"

Start by making a comprehensive list of everything you need to do. Writing it down helps you gain clarity and realize that the list isn't as overwhelming as it may seem when it's swirling around in your mind. If it feels too daunting, you can focus on one specific area, such as work deliverables or personal tasks. Break things down if necessary so there are clearly defined, practicable chunks that you can actually accomplish.

Once you have your list, identify priority tasks based on either:

1. Any looming deadlines or
2. The potential for that task to impact other tasks or else bring benefits

Tasks that satisfy both the above conditions can be identified as frogs. Of course, tasks should actually align with your goals and values (use a little Spartan minimalism to confirm whether you need to do it at all).

Now, the next morning when you wake up, you know you have a date with your frog. Eating a frog is disgusting, so don't draw it out and make it last longer than it needs to. In fact, your approach should be to fling yourself at the task with high energy and extreme motivation. Swallow that frog so quickly and so completely that you barely taste it going down! Then you can relax, take a look at the rest of your day, and move on with ease—the opposite of that feeling of dread and avoidance you get had you procrastinated, knowing that the frog was waiting for you . . .

Step 2: Eat the biggest frog first

Unless you are the president of a country or an action movie hero, you probably won't have more than one *really* big frog a day. If there are two frogs, eat the biggest one first and ignore the other one until you've done so.

You might need to do a little frog triage. Sort your tasks according to two factors:

1. How important it is
2. How likely you are to try to avoid it

If a task is very important and you are likely to try to delay and resist it, then that makes it a big frog you should eat ASAP. Literally identify the task you are most dreading and most want to procrastinate and put it at the front of the line.

Step 3: Eat your frogs in the morning, then do everything else

To optimize productivity, tackle your "frogs" in the morning. After going through your morning routine, make it a priority to engage with the most challenging task right away. **Once completed**, you can shift your focus to less critical tasks. By successfully tackling the difficult task, you've already made significant progress and set a positive tone for the rest of the day. You may find you actually fire yourself up and feel *more* motivated to blast through other tasks. Since the most challenging task is already behind you, you'll be confident in your own abilities. Nothing feels as good as having completed a major task before 10 a.m.

You Need Good Goals

Before we move on, it's worth noting that you should obviously only be eating those frogs that genuinely will move you toward a goal that is of real value to you. It's no use forcing yourself to tackle challenging tasks if those tasks do not contribute meaningfully to a goal, or if the goal you've identified was not appropriate in the first place.

Here's a quick checklist to make sure your goals are as they should be:

- Goals should be SMART—are they specific, measurable, achievable, relevant, and time-bound? If not, they may need to be re-formulated until you know with crystal clarity what the goal is, how you'll know when you've achieved it, how it relates to your life in general, and the deadline you're giving yourself.

- What is the context of these goals? Zoom in and out again to get a clear sense of your long term, mid-term and short-term goals. Where does this task fit?

- Stay connected to meaning, purpose, and values. What is your Big Why behind all of it? How does this goal help you be the kind of person you want to be? Are you tapping into this genuine motivation, or are you going through the motions and achieving a generic goal that somebody else told you was important? People change, and their values change, too. It's okay to abandon a dream for something else as you grow and evolve.

- What is your priority? If you have more than one, then you don't have any! Select the *single* most important task and goal for you right now. Make sure that you're not getting distracted or bogged down in unnecessary detail.

The First Pancake Theory

If you've ever made pancakes, you'll know about the theory that your first one is always a bit of a mess. Once you've warmed up, the therapy goes, the rest of your pancakes are usually fine. The "first pancake theory" says that productivity is a little like this: Your first task of the day is always a write-off, so, contrary to the frog technique, you *don't* want to schedule your most important task for this time.

While these approaches look to be opposites on the surface, they are actually highly compatible. A bad first pancake does not mean the entire batch will be bad. Skilled chefs understand this and do not get discouraged by a less-than-perfect pancake. They just make the first bad pancake and move on. They acknowledge it as part of the process and make enough batter to allow for a test or gauge to determine what adjustments are needed for subsequent pancakes.

Instead of expecting perfection right from the start, the theory suggests embracing imperfections and considering them throwaways or learning opportunities. But in its own way, this embracing of initial imperfection **is** the frog. Often, what we procrastinate with and avoid is that awkward beginner stage when we're not yet confident in our abilities, unclear on our strategy, or just way out of our comfort zone. We're starting with a cold frying pan.

People who balk at the idea of rushing into a difficult task first thing in the morning need not worry. For them, that small initial baby step may be the "frog." It's a little like the pre-game approach described above. You start a task without spooking yourself and without feeling as though you have even started. You get comfortable with the fact that you'll need a little warm-up before you gradually build momentum.

However you envision your tasks, however, a few things remain the same: It's worth observing your attitude and your blind spots and devising a way forward that leverages those things in your favor. If you're really not a morning person, you don't *have to* do the most difficult task in the morning—but absolutely do it when you're most energetic, whenever that may be. If you would find it psychologically easier to just get started with a task rather than do it as quickly as possible, then do that, if it works for you.

The onus is on you to experiment and adjust according to the results you achieve. Sadly, there is no way to arrange your affairs where you don't have to occasionally push yourself past your own inertia, fear, or hesitancy. It's just a question of finding out what will sincerely be the best approach to do that.

Warren Buffett's Two-List Strategy

If all this talk of pancakes and frogs does nothing for you, you might like to introduce elements from Warren Buffett's "two-list" technique. You might find it especially useful if you're a very ambitious type who always has several plans and projects going at one time.

It involves making a list of twenty-five career goals and then selecting the top five most important ones. The remaining twenty goals are considered the "avoid at all costs" list, meaning they receive *no attention* until the top five goals have been achieved. This approach emphasizes focusing on the most critical objectives and prioritizing them above all else.

Step One: List the top twenty-five goals. Take your time to compile a comprehensive list of twenty-five goals you would like to accomplish in your lifetime. Start with a larger time frame and then narrow it down to a specific period, such as one year, to make it more manageable.

Step Two: Choose the five most important goals. Select the five most significant goals from your list of twenty-five. Imagine that you can only accomplish these five in your life, and prioritize accordingly. Circle them and move on to the next step.

Step Three: Create two lists, Divide your goals into two lists. List A consists of your top five goals, which become your exclusive focus. List B includes the remaining twenty goals and should be seen as a "avoid at all costs" list until you have achieved all the goals on List A.

Step Four: After completing the top five, repeat the process. Once you have accomplished the goals on List A, start the process again. Create a new list of twenty-five goals and prioritize them. Avoid working on the goals from List B until you have succeeded with the primary five. You may, of course, find that things have moved on in the meantime, and those earlier goals are no longer quite as relevant.

The key is to prioritize and focus on a small number of goals at a time, maximizing the effectiveness of your time and energy. By avoiding distractions and maintaining a clear focus on your top goals, you increase your chances of success. So, in a way, Buffett is all about making *everything* on your to-do list a frog! From his point of view, there really is no point in doing anything other than the most important task (and the Spartans would likely agree with him!). Then, you don't even waste time deciding what is and isn't your priority. You only care about your priority, end of story.

There are countless other hacks, tricks, techniques, and methods that are designed to help you streamline your to-do list and get you working with maximum efficiency every day. But most of them rely on the very basic premise that **it's always better to frontload effort and to do the big, important, difficult thing first.**

Don't take the present moment for granted. You cannot guarantee what the future will bring, and you cannot rely on having more motivation, time, money, etc. in the future than you do now. There is a quote from the Yoga Vasistha: **"There is no greater power than right action in the present moment.**" That is all we have, in fact. The present moment and the power to *choose* the right action.

Never Zero Commitment

As we near the end of this book, we'll finish on what is perhaps a surprising conclusion: Motivation and self-discipline are not *that* important.

If we follow the habits and mindsets of people who have truly mastered their own lives and achieved their dreams, we will find that they are not necessarily workaholics or madly ambitious. Rather, they are **committed**—and this is different from merely being motivated.

When you are committed, you act because you have decided you will act.

Motivation is irrelevant.

Inspiration is irrelevant.

Your mood, the time of day, the weather, other people's actions—all irrelevant.

You have decided that you will act in accordance with your goal, and so you do that. You are dedicated, and you simply do not recognize anything as a legitimate cause to give up on that. There is something clarifying about commitment. There is zero wiggle room, zero potential to weasel in an excuse. When you commit, you make a promise to yourself that you will act *no matter what*. And in a way, that keeps things extremely simple.

It doesn't matter if you are completely bored out of your mind, exhausted, unmotivated, doubtful, terrified, confused, ashamed, or disinterested. You act because you said you would. You have made a promise to yourself, and you intend to maintain your own good name and reputation . . . with yourself.

You're probably wondering how this steely resolve works in the face of the inevitable adversity and setbacks we discussed earlier. There is a proverb that says, "It doesn't matter how slow you walk, only don't stop." This is the spirit behind the concept of never zero commitment, which emphasizes **setting a minimum acceptable version of a habit and committing to it for a specific period of time without fail**. It is about taking full responsibility and control of your life, leaving no room for excuses.

Let's say you wake up one morning and can't face the idea of your daily run. In fact, you feel yourself coming down with a cold. But you *don't* simply abandon your overall mission to have more discipline and more physical fitness in your life. You do what you can, which in this case means going for a gentle walk outside. What if you can't even manage a gentle walk? Then you do an even gentler indoor walkabout for ten minutes. Basically, no matter what, doing nothing is simply not an option for you.

Your commitment remains one hundred percent, even though your ability to act will waver over time.

Your goal is to give your best in each moment. Some days, your best will be amazing; other days your best will barely amount to anything. Keep a hold of your firm commitment, however, and it doesn't matter. You are still on your path.

Rather than trying to implement never zero commitment for every habit, first focus on just one or two keystone habits that will significantly contribute to your goals. Examples could include daily meditation for five minutes, dedicating a specific time slot for writing each day for a defined period, expressing appreciation to your partner before going to sleep until the end of the year, studying Spanish for twenty minutes daily until your trip to Spain, or abstaining from beer or sweets until after a marathon.

By mastering the never zero commitment strategy in one area, you develop the skill of self-discipline, making it easier to incorporate additional habits into your routine. As each habit becomes integrated, you can then expand your commitment to other aspects of your life. This approach allows you to build momentum and progressively enhance your self-discipline.

When making Never Zero commitments, take note of these three elements: Make your commitments timely, small, and uncompromising.

Timely Commitment: Making a never zero commitment is a significant step toward building self-discipline and achieving your goals. It requires choosing a specific start date and duration for your commitment. This start date should be marked on your calendar or kept in a visible place as a reminder of the new beginning you're working toward.

The time commitment can vary based on your goal, ranging from a few days or weeks to a lifetime commitment. For essential habits or breaking addictions, committing for a lifetime may be appropriate. The never zero commitment focuses your energy, eliminates excuses, and leaves no option for failure.

It's important to start with a manageable commitment if you're new to the never zero approach. Begin with a smaller goal, such as being sugar-free for ten days or facing social anxiety daily for three weeks. Stick to the commitment without making excuses. After the set time, you can reassess and decide whether to continue with another never zero sprint, adjust the time commitment, or make it a permanent part of your life.

Small Commitment: When making a never zero commitment, it is important to start small and avoid being overly ambitious. If you're new to a habit, don't set unrealistic expectations or put excessive pressure on yourself. Beginning with a small commitment helps you avoid stress, disappointment, and frustration.

What's crucial is staying consistent and not giving up, regardless of how small the commitment may be. Progressing slowly is fine; what matters is following through on your decision as if it's a matter of life or death.

However, there is an exception for "not to do" commitments, such as quitting smoking or drinking alcohol. In these cases, going cold turkey and completely abstaining may be more effective than trying moderation. Accepting a temporary period of difficulty can lead to long-term success in breaking the addiction.

Uncompromising Commitment: Take action without excuses during your designated never zero commitment period. No matter the circumstances or how you feel, stay true to your commitment. Whether you're doubtful, fearful, in pain, confused, or lacking motivation, push through and take action.

If you are trying to complete your novel, then your never zero commitment to yourself may simply be to make sure you write at least *one* word a day. Sounds ridiculously small, but psychologically this works. Come to an agreement with yourself that you will never write zero words, ever. Even if you've had a disaster of a day and no time to sit down and write, you can still work on your novel and add just a single word, right?

In the real world, though, you seldom have to push things this far. You may sit down to do that word and manage a sentence. And if you've done a sentence, you may as well complete a paragraph. The great thing about this approach is that some days you will produce a lot, and some days you will just keep your productivity engine ticking over. Both things are important.

Mentally tell yourself that there is a bare minimum that you will always achieve, every day, rain or shine. This could align with your "pre-game routine" or be that first imperfect pancake that needs to be done before you can carry on with the others. It's up to you what your commitment is, but rest in the fact that once you've made it, that's it. There's nothing more to think about—just do it.

Summary:

- Long-term discipline means understanding that adversity and challenge will arise and are part of the process. The question is whether you work with your limits or against them. Moderate your expectations and be comfortable with the fact of difficulty at some point in the future.

- Timing is the key, and the rest is non-negotiable. Moderation and proper planning around natural cycles are actually smarter, more effective, and more elegant than ignoring your limits. Try to plan your activities around your ultradian rhythms, which run approximately on a roughly ninety-minute cycle. Do deep work and take real breaks at the right moment.

- It's normal for motivation levels to rise and fall. Your pre-game routine helps you maintain good habits despite these fluctuations. Self-discipline doesn't mean it gets easier; it means we get stronger. A pre-game routine should be easy, automatic, active, and practiced consistently every day to entrench it. The hardest part is starting!

- A great rule to live by is: do the big thing first. Prioritize any looming deadlines and tasks that you're most likely to avoid, then do them first in the morning or when you're most alert and energized. If you need to get the bad "first pancake" out of the way first, then do that. What matters is focused, strategic action. Finally, Warren Buffett's two-list technique asks you to *only* focus on those five goals that are a priority for you, and forget everything else. However you approach it, it's always better to frontload effort and to do the big, important, difficult thing first.

- Never zero commitment means setting a minimum acceptable version of a habit and committing to it for a specific period of time without fail. Simply commit to never letting yourself make no effort toward your goal—then motivation and inspiration become irrelevant.

Summary Guide

CHAPTER ONE: "WHAT'S WRONG WITH ME?!"

- Laziness can be defined as the conscious unwillingness to put in the necessary effort required for a task, encompassing both mental and physical exertion. It's a cluster of behaviors, beliefs, attitudes, habits, and emotions, and acts as a trigger for secondary behaviors, thoughts, and feelings.

- Different types (or rather, causes) of laziness include confusion (I don't know what to do), fear (I can't do it), a fixed rather than growth mindset (I can't fail), fatigue (I'm too tired), apathy (I don't care), low self-belief (I'm just a lazy person; I can't do it), so-called "loss of heart" (What difference does it make, anyway?), and comfort orientation, or the preference for ease over effort (I'll do it . . . after I do this other fun thing).

- Your reason for procrastination (or mix of reasons) will determine what course of action you take to fix the problem. You may need more discipline, or to take a break, shift your mindset, reassess your goals, or work on time or energy management.

- The Shaolin monks have a similar model of "five hindrances to self-mastery," which include sensual desire, ill will, sloth and torpor, restlessness (distraction), and doubt/skepticism. Their overarching solution for most laziness problems is not discipline, but self-mastery.

- You can remove the obstacles on your path using the RAIN method, which stands for recognize, accept, investigate, and non-identification. Become aware of your experience, accept it completely, inquire into its nature, and ensure you have some psychological distance so you can make conscious choices moving forward.

- What both models recognize is that *experiential avoidance* is at the heart of much laziness and procrastination. Adversity and discomfort are normal in life, but when we avoid them, we prolong our problems. Acceptance is the easy way out and entails not adding "second darts" to discomfort. The quicker you can accept pain, the quicker you can move on from it without turning it into suffering.

CHAPTER TWO: THE DISCIPLINE MINDSET

- Actions matter, but what's important is the attitude and mindset behind those actions.
- Three things characterize the mindsets of people with motivation, discipline, and effectiveness in life: the ability to embrace and work with discomfort, psychological flexibility, and a capacity for emotional self-regulation.
- There is an unavoidable connection between discomfort and growth, so growth requires getting familiar with discomfort. Comfort creep explains that the easier we make our lives, the less able we are to tolerate things that are not easy. One solution is to deliberately introduce and embrace discomfort in your life—for example, with cold showers, hard physical activity, or embracing boredom.
- Psychological flexibility is the ability to continually take action in accordance with one's values, despite change, uncertainty, and distress. It can be cultivated using the ACT approach, where you stay focused on what you value no matter what negative or uncomfortable sensations arise.
- ACT skills include accepting all emotional responses, defusing and detaching from

that experience, remaining anchored in the present, staying connected to your values, perspective switching, and choosing committed action on your own terms.

- The ninety-second rule of emotional control teaches us that "when a person has a reaction to something in their environment, there's a ninety-second chemical process that happens; any remaining emotional response is just the person choosing to stay in that emotional loop." Knowing this, we can choose our response beyond the ninety seconds. Get to know your triggers, label your emotions as they arise, and accept them.

CHAPTER THREE: THE DISCIPLINE HABIT

- It's possible to harness your mind power and use it to work for you, rather than constantly living at its mercy, or even having it work against you.
- People tend to procrastinate because they don't feel like they are in the right mood to complete the task, and they believe that their mood will change in the near future. But this sets up a procrastination "doom loop" that continuously reinforces itself.

Perfectionism, fear of success/failure, and a powerless mindset all exacerbate the problem.

- To get out of the loop requires plenty of self-compassion, learning how to reframe our thinking around the task (focus on values, not shortcomings), and taking small, meaningful steps toward our goal. It's about mood and energy management, not time management or organization.

- Your attention operates in three modes: flashlight (orienting system), caution sign (alerting system), and juggler (executive functioning). To master self-discipline, develop the mindfulness skill of noticing when your attentional flashlight has wandered away from the task at hand, and bring it gently back without judgment.

- The arrow model of focus explains the role of epinephrine, acetylcholine, and dopamine in driving, focusing, and sustaining our attentional awareness, respectively. To improve self-discipline, increase/modulate these levels using meditation and visualization techniques, "good stress," caffeine, and healthy lifestyle choices.

- Finally, the Spartans can teach us about discipline by subtraction rather than addition, i.e., what we choose not to focus on. Think carefully about what is irrelevant or harmful, and void those tasks. You have finite resources, so be strategic with them and simplify—if you do so, there will be enough time and energy to achieve your dreams.

CHAPTER FOUR: SELF-DISCIPLINE, TODAY AND FOREVER

- Long-term discipline means understanding that adversity and challenge will arise and are part of the process. The question is whether you work with your limits or against them. Moderate your expectations and be comfortable with the fact of difficulty at some point in the future.
- Timing is the key, and the rest is non-negotiable. Moderation and proper planning around natural cycles are actually smarter, more effective, and more elegant than ignoring your limits. Try to plan your activities around your ultradian rhythms, which run approximately on a roughly ninety-minute cycle. Do deep work and take real breaks at the right moment.

- It's normal for motivation levels to rise and fall. Your pre-game routine helps you maintain good habits despite these fluctuations. Self-discipline doesn't mean it gets easier; it means we get stronger. A pre-game routine should be easy, automatic, active, and practiced consistently every day to entrench it. The hardest part is starting!

- A great rule to live by is: do the big thing first. Prioritize any looming deadlines and tasks that you're most likely to avoid, then do them first in the morning or when you're most alert and energized. If you need to get the bad "first pancake" out of the way first, then do that. What matters is focused, strategic action. Finally, Warren Buffett's two-list technique asks you to *only* focus on those five goals that are a priority for you, and forget everything else. However you approach it, it's always better to frontload effort and to do the big, important, difficult thing first.

- Never zero commitment means setting a minimum acceptable version of a habit and committing to it for a specific period of time without fail. Simply commit to never letting yourself make no effort toward your goal—then motivation and inspiration become irrelevant.

9 781647 435189